DAN QUAYLE

WORTH FIGHTING FOR

WORD PUBLISHING

NASHVILLE

A Thomas Nelson Company

Published in association with Sealy M. Yates, literary agent, Orange, California.

Book design by Mark McGarry
Set in Fairfield

Library of Congress Cataloging-in-Publication Data
Quayle, Dan, 1947–
    Worth fighting for / by Dan Quayle.
        p. cm
    ISBN 0–8499–1602–2
    1. United States—Politics and government—1993–
    2. United States—Social conditions—1980– . I. Title.
E885-Q39   1999
973.929—dc21   99–29541
                                                    CIP

Printed in the United States of America.
99 00 01 02 03 04 BVG 9 8 7 6 5 4 3 2 1

To Marilyn, Tucker, Benjamin, and Corinne

Contents

Preface

My 1994 memoir, *Standing Firm*, ended with the assertion, "I have much yet to do." This book lays out in detail what I think the next president must do.

Since leaving the vice presidency in 1993, I have moved twice, first from Washington, D.C., to Indianapolis, and then from Indianapolis to Phoenix. This latter move came about because Marilyn and I wanted to be close to my parents as my father's health began to fail.

I've also watched my household shrink. Two of my children have graduated from college—Tucker from Lehigh and Ben from Duke. My youngest, Corinne, is also gone from the house most of the year as she nears the end of her undergraduate studies. Tucker is working in China with a multinational company, and Ben has been accepted to law school. We watch our children's lives with the same mixture of pride and wonder that all parents feel.

While family has been my highest priority, I've also been busy on many other fronts. I've written two previous books, helped found an investment company, sat on several corporate boards, served as a trustee of the Hudson Institute, and taught graduate business students the realities of competitive politics. The teaching experience has perhaps been the most enjoyable of all. I taught for two years at Thunderbird, the American Graduate School of International Management. About one-third of the students were from abroad. Thunderbird, like many business schools, requires its students to acquire some work experience between their undergraduate and graduate studies. As a result, my students were not only dedicated and smart, they had also been in the real world of work for at least a few years.

These students were deeply interested in the course and the reading, but some of them displayed a genuine discontent with politics itself. Like many people in our country, they are simply turned off by politics, choosing not to participate at all in the selection of our leaders. This is true in the coffee shops of Main Street and in living rooms throughout America. Reversing this decline in civic participation is a huge challenge for the nation.

When book deadlines and classroom commitments have allowed, I have also spent a good part of the past six years traveling to support men and women who are struggling to keep America true to its highest principles and its founding ideals. Marilyn and I have crisscrossed the country to support causes and candidates pledged to the principles of freedom, faith, and family. That has meant a lot of time in airplanes and hotels, but we have been happy to work as hard as we could to make a difference.

Unfortunately, the efforts we and millions of others have made have been only partly successful. Often we have worked in vain. America on the eve of a new century is much coarser than it was a decade ago and increasingly transfixed by profits and portfolios.

Astonishingly, many people think the only statistic that matters is the gross domestic product. Increasingly, American elites appear willing to leave large numbers of their fellow citizens behind as the stock market lifts them into higher income brackets.

I am not.

Earlier this year I gave a talk in Manchester, New Hampshire, where I discussed my unease with a culture absorbed in its own net worth even as many millions are working harder and longer—and still feeling that they are barely coping with bills and all the demands of family and community. I explained that I saw an America in cultural decline even as its surface prosperity dazzled the world. I also noted that the pillars of American security—military preparedness and a common attachment to shared ideals—were badly damaged.

A woman came up through the crowd to thank me and to tell me that she sensed in my remarks something different from what she had heard from a dozen presidential candidates she had encountered in the past. What she sensed is that my campaign is rooted in the reality of America on the brink of the twenty-first century. I've started a business, hassled with health insurance carriers, arranged for the long-term care of an infirm parent, and watched my children react to the culture around them. Mixed into these ordinary experiences of life have been some extraordinary opportunities to meet with leaders in the international business and political communities. Three times, for example, I have visited China and met that country's senior leaders, including President Jiang Zemin and Premier Zhu Rongi.

In sum, even as my life since January 1993 has been very much like yours, it has also been a period of continuing engagement in the world of international events.

It would have been easy to stay on the sidelines and enjoy the undeniable benefits of being a former vice president. I suppose I could have continued my service on corporate boards, played in a pro-am golf tournament every week, and generally eased into the new decade in a position of comfort and relative security.

I simply cannot do that. I care deeply about this country and its people in a way that midwesterners have always done: openly and unashamedly. That love will not allow me to sit out the most important campaign in a generation. Not since 1980 have the stakes been this high. Because I unhesitatingly urge my children and students to involve themselves in the effort to guide America's future, so I am compelled to do the same. And that means running for president.

The challenges ahead are hugely complex but also, in a real way, very simple. The reading I assign my classes underscores the complexity, whether it's I. M. Destler's *American Trade Politics,* Richard Bernstein and Ross H. Munro's *The Coming Conflict with China,* Hedrick Smith's *The Power Game,* Kenneth T. Walsh's *Feeding the Beast,* or any of several other titles. The demands of politics, economics, and national security combine to make America's difficulties seem almost intractable. But I am continually refreshed by my constant encounters with real Americans who are working, often without pay or recognition, to resolve the country's most pressing problems. That's the simple truth: America's greatness continues to reside not in her wealth or her military prowess but in her wonderful people.

I am willing to run this race with all of its challenges, its promise of fatigue, and its certainty of low blows and cheap shots, because millions of Americans are trying to return this country to its highest calling. Even as a few voices have called it quits and urged a retreat from a political arena that they regard as beyond repair, still the rest of us must continue the effort to hold America to its ideals.

Because so many Americans are willing to sacrifice their time and their comforts, so am I. Because you are willing to study the platforms and promises of candidates, I am willing to spell mine out in these pages. And because we are all given opportunities to advance the country's future now and for the next generation, I will not waste mine.

That is why I am proud and honored to be a candidate for the presidency of the United States of America. And I guarantee you that if I win, you will never have occasion to regret the support I am asking of you and that I hope you will generously give.

DAN QUAYLE

PART 1

America at a Crossroads

The Presidency is not merely an administrative office. . . . It is pre-eminently a place of moral leadership. All our great Presidents were leaders of thought at times when certain historic ideas in the life of the nation had to be clarified.

—FRANKLIN D. ROOSEVELT

1

The Next American Century

WILL THE twenty-first century come to be known as another "American century"? If we choose wisely, the answer is yes. This is our challenge. In these one hundred years just ending, America's greatness provided the margin of victory in the First World War, the overwhelming force behind victory in the Second World War, and the patient endurance and purpose that ultimately triumphed in the Cold War. Today, America is the only genuine superpower. We are number one militarily, economically, and technologically. Our influence on the world is unprecedented. On top of these achievements we are enjoying a stunning level of material wealth that was not imagined even a generation ago.

Moreover, the situation of the American people is unique. Other powers have risen in the past. Various empires have dominated at different times in history. But never has a single power fueled by freedom achieved so much. Other empires have ruled because of superior military force. Only America has triumphed because of its ideals, and central to these ideals has been freedom.

Today, that freedom is eroding. It is eroding because the values that allowed it to flourish are everywhere in retreat. As our amazing prosperity has begun to anesthetize us to our peril, petty tyrants around the world are watching our slow descent into confusion about who we are and what we value. Our world leadership is now routinely mocked. It will not be long before it is challenged.

We have to ask ourselves: Do we genuinely believe in America as a special nation, one that ought to cherish and guard its place as protector not only of the freedom of its people but of the stability of the globe? If we do intend for the new century to be another American century, then three fundamental challenges must be faced, and three crucial choices must be made.

First, we must understand that the values that built this country and molded a people strong enough to survive as a free people are under attack, and we must choose to reclaim them.

Second, we must understand that American prosperity depends most of all upon the country's vast middle class, a middle class that flourishes only with freedom. Thus we must choose to protect it from the extraordinary appetite of the huge and growing federal government, an insatiable appetite continually demanding more in taxes as it gnaws away at the people's freedom. We must remember that America's promise to the poorest among us is that they can, in no more than a generation, join that middle class.

And finally, we must clearly understand that America will either lead the world, or it will be attacked again and again and will eventually suffer. We need to summon the courage to claim our place as the lone superpower and to defend that status without apology, for it is no more than the natural result of our values and the freedom those values have made possible. In other words, we must freely pick up and carry the burden of our world leadership. To do so is both in America's best interest and in the world's as well.

We need to do a number of things and do them very quickly.

To secure peace and prosperity, America must boldly assume the responsibility of leadership lest we reach the point of international disorder from which recovery will be impossible without enormous cost in the lives of the next generation. America must export not just goods but the message of freedom and human dignity that will bring hope to people everywhere.

To secure the blessings of liberty at home, we must raise our sights and seek a higher level of growth so that no American is left behind. We must rescue the middle class from a crushing burden of taxation and the demands of a nanny state that threatens to intrude into every aspect of our lives.

We must once again proudly hold up freedom as the guardian of hope and opportunity. The freedom I am referring to is freedom of faith and speech, freedom of choice in how we bring up and educate our children, freedom to arrange our golden years. We have by now become quite numbed to the incursions that government makes into our daily lives. We have to wake up and take back the freedom that our parents and grandparents once cherished and defended.

Our first task, however, is to end any confusion about what we value most. We have leaders who have placed personal gain over personal honor and self-interest over the national welfare. The Clinton-Gore team has celebrated obstruction and lying, and it has embraced those who, since the 1960s, have ceaselessly pounded away at honor, duty, country, and the rule of law, routinely trashing as outdated and hopelessly quaint the values the rest of us hold dear.

To strengthen the moral fabric of our country, we must reclaim the values of faith in God, integrity, responsibility, courage, thrift, and industry. Without these virtues we will become merely another country in just another century, having squandered our priceless legacy.

Billy Graham has remarked that America is a long way down the wrong road, and he's right. But it's not a hopeless situation. The country is like a hiker lost in a deep woods. Before he stumbles even deeper into trouble, he's got to stop, take a long look around, and consult his compass.

We are in that ominous forest, all right, and it is a confusing place. For there are now two Americas. One America is largely upper or upper-middle class. Its inhabitants make so much money that they have no idea how great the pressures have grown on the middle class in America. The elites simply can't relate to those who struggle to make ends meet. They are, for instance, quite unconscious of the difference that a thousand dollars can make in the life of an ordinary American family. They are equally indifferent to the peeling plaster and incoherent lesson plans of America's urban public schools because their children are educated at private schools in safe places. They have never heard the sound of gunfire in their streets, so they cannot comprehend the demand of citizens of the other America for safety, both in the call for more police and in the form of gun ownership.

America must choose, and the choice could not be more stark: a country by and for the elite, or a country that honors its middle class and gives real hope to those who struggle to become part of it. By honoring the virtues of that second America, Ronald Reagan unleashed the nation's productive capacity and triggered a new surge of American confidence. His leadership undeniably led to the defeat of communism and set the stage for unparalleled prosperity, yet others have tried to take the credit. Children of the sixties have come to power and, not for the first time, have laid claim to an unearned honor. Bill Clinton and Al Gore have shamelessly taken credit for the prosperity they inherited and for an American dominance on the globe they have undermined. When Gore gave himself credit for "creating the Internet" he unconsciously revealed the arrogance of those who confuse their roles as bystanders with the hard work of the entrepeneurs who made it all possible. Many of today's powerful elite cut their teeth in the hubris of the sixties and in the ensuing years have learned nothing of the virtue of humility. They claim as their achievement all that sparkles, and all that is poisoned they lay at the feet of ordinary Americans who honor faith and family.

Moreover, they have strenuously resisted any attempt to answer the crucial questions about the course of the country. The Clinton-Gore administration is even proud of its poll and focus group–driven policies, which are long—very long—on talk, but short on vision.

For many years after World War II, our country enjoyed a remarkable consensus on the most important issue facing it: namely, the threat of Soviet imperialism. We recognized that if we did not resist the Soviets' aggression, they would do to other countries what they had done to Eastern Europe following the war, to Hungary in 1956, and to Czechoslovakia in 1968. There was bipartisan support for devoting the resources necessary to protect America and the free world from Soviet expansionism. Unfortunately, this consensus about American purpose was shattered by the Vietnam War.

In 1972, the McGovern campaign introduced into American politics a cadre of political activists who held America to be a mixed blessing at best. Ronald Reagan and the coalition he led stood in firm opposition to the "blame America first" crowd. He recognized the stark choices America confronted in the world. When Reagan labeled the Soviet Union "the evil empire," the self-anointed recoiled from his candor, but the country did not. When he drew a sharp distinction between the Republican and Democratic Parties on matters such as the proper size and scope of government, the burden of taxation, and the requirements of national security, he spoke over the heads of the media elite and directly to the majority of Americans. And that majority provided him with two landslide mandates.

In the decade since President Reagan left office, not only have the Democrats remade their image without remaking their philosophy, but they have done so without challenge from the Republicans. The irony is that the Clinton-Gore administration has been as relentlessly ideological as George McGovern's would ever have been.

First, in foreign affairs, where America ought to lead, they have abdicated. The current administration's incompetence on foreign policy matters is so widely remarked upon that many seem now to assume that America could never lead, that it can only "partner." The ill-advised entry into the Yugoslavian civil war is only the latest example of a confused, ad hoc foreign policy.

Second, on cultural issues—the morality of the country and the centrality of the family—the administration has opposed much that is traditional, much that is normal, much that is mainstream. Whether it was vetoing partial-birth abortion legislation, advancing gays in the military, pursuing the environmental extremism of Al Gore, attempting a government takeover of healthcare, or proposing that the federal government control private-sector companies through social security trust fund investments, the core agenda of the Clinton-Gore administration has been at the leftward fringe of politics.

They relentlessly promote their leftist agenda, but never out loud, and always camouflage it in the rhetoric of "strengthening the community" and "helping the children."

Instead of uniting Americans, Bill Clinton and Al Gore have

sought to divide and confuse by abusing the power of the bully pulpit. It is now routine to hear self-anointed guardians of the country's "moderate center" denounce as "extreme and intolerant" ordinary Americans defending ordinary traditions. One of the worst instances of this effort to marginalize the mainstream followed the tragic bombing of the Oklahoma City federal building. As Americans grieved with the victims and their families, Bill Clinton chose to suggest that those who argued for small government and a limited federal role had somehow contributed to a climate of hate that propelled the criminal psyche of Timothy McVeigh. Their debasement of rhetoric did not end there. Only last year Al Gore declared that Republicans opposed "statistical" sampling in the census because the GOP did not want to count African Americans. That was an obscene lie.

Time and time again, the Clinton-Gore administration has gone "Orwellian." They proclaim that "the era of big government is over" while the total of federal tax receipts reaches the highest level recorded in American history. They lambaste school vouchers as "an irresponsible assault" on public education, yet send their children to elite private schools far removed from mainstream America and its struggles with public education. They consistently label tax cut proposals as "risky schemes" that threaten social security, yet offer no solution to the obvious problems we face in preserving social security for future generations. They roll out the attack ads about "slashing Medicare," ignoring the fact—documented by their own budget figures—that Medicare spending has increased every year under Republican leadership.

Most of the time, the media report the fictions as true.

So be it. Our challenge is to put our agenda concisely and consistently before the American people. A new generation of Americans must be encouraged to set aside their cynicism and again take up the commitment to public service.

We Americans have become dangerously nonchalant when it comes to politics. More and more people are saying that elections do not matter, and fewer among us are contesting that cynicism.

But elections *do* matter, and now more than ever the stakes are very high.

It is not just that the next president is likely to appoint three Supreme Court justices or that the next administration will face entirely new challenges on the global stage. In the next election we will be making a number of crucial choices:

We will choose between personal freedom and a vast and growing government.

We will choose to cut taxes or to leave them at their historically high levels.

We will choose to build a ballistic missile defense or to leave ourselves vulnerable to nuclear blackmail.

We will choose to shake up the education establishment and demand excellence in education for all our children or to force another generation of young people to remain in failing and sometimes downright dangerous schools.

We will choose a culture that embraces, celebrates, and protects life or one in which violence, crime, and drug use are accepted as a given and death is just a choice.

We will choose to be a country of one people working together for the common good or to be a collection of independent interests competing with each other for political or social power.

It's time to choose. We cheer our small victories on one or another issue, but we forget that these victories are largely holding actions.

We are in the same condition now as in March 1863, when Lincoln called for a day of fasting and repentance. "We have forgotten God," wrote the father of the Republican Party. "Intoxicated with unbroken success, we have become too self-sufficient to feel the necessity of redeeming and preserving grace, too proud to pray to the God that made us!"

The next election must reset our moral compass. We must understand that "prosperity" without values is no prosperity at all.

PART 2

The Cultural Divide

When freedom does not have a purpose, when it does not wish to know anything about the rule of law engraved in the hearts of men and women, when it does not listen to the voice of conscience, it turns against humanity and society.

—POPE JOHN PAUL II

2

Values Matter Most

A SECOND American century requires, first and foremost, a restoration of the values that have molded our national character. These values came under an across-the-board assault in the sixties, and they continue to be ridiculed and mocked today.

I want to be clear about our objective. A restoration of values means understanding that there are some universal truths, some constants. Each person does not have the right to invent a value system and pass it off as good for the rest of society. As Margaret Thatcher has warned, "Just as there are physical laws which we break at our peril, so there are moral laws which, if we flout them, will lead to personal and national decline."

A restoration of values is also properly viewed as a defense against those who wish to use big government to impose their own beliefs on the rest of us. The left has done an effective job of casting this debate in exactly the opposite terms, and it is time we set it straight. Perhaps most important, we must, and I intend to, explain why defending these values is the best hope we have for an educated citizenry, a society that contains communities and families—not interest groups and ethnic division—a country at peace with itself.

Two years ago, I gave a speech in North Carolina on behalf of a scholarship fund that my friend Billy Prim had created for underprivileged students. Among the listeners that night was a waitress working her second job. She was a hardworking, concerned parent. After my remarks, she approached me with a story. Her second-grade daughter's classmate had a sister, fourteen, who had given birth to twins. The daughter's teacher had called on the class to have a round of applause when the birth was announced. "Mr. Quayle," said the waitress, "do something!"

I do not for a moment believe that this waitress was condemning the teenage mother or even the teacher. What inspired her passion seemed to me to be a feeling that no matter how hard she worked the world was spinning beyond her control. Her most precious possession—her daughter—was caught up in a culture where a fourteen-year-old having twins was an event that called for applause. Her values—the values she wished to pass to her daughter—were under assault.

Syndicated columnist Ben Wattenberg wrote a fine book in 1996 from which I borrowed the title of this chapter: *Values Matter Most*. Wattenberg has traveled this country posing the question: Which is the bigger challenge facing America, jobs or values? I borrowed his question and have for the past three years been posing it to people across the country. Both Wattenberg and I have found that the vast majority always answers, "Values." The chorus of Americans concerned with this country's values is large and growing, and it is finally finding its voice.

There are deep, if not irreconcilable, differences between left and right on the issue of the country's core values. The *Murphy Brown* speech I gave in 1992 was notable because it clearly demonstrated that the divide existed. Nothing has changed since then, though more have joined me in recognizing it. If anything, the divide has grown deeper.

Let me give you one example. I have known since early 1998 that I would soon be writing this book. I wanted to detail what I've introduced in the previous chapter: namely, the direction America must now take and the leadership needed to do it. So I prepared an outline and circulated it to various publishers, including publishing giant Random House. The president and editor-in-chief of Random House, Ann Godoff, received and reviewed the synopsis. Here, in its entirety, is her written response to my agent:

> Mr. Quayle's arguments will set his agenda squarely before the American people. The proposal is well thought through. The trouble is I just don't want to be party to the promulgation of ideas I disagree with so profoundly. In the end, I think, the best publishing is done without reservation.
>
> Best,
Ann

She, of course, had the right to reject this book. But as you read these pages, ask yourself what it is that so "profoundly" troubled the editor-in-chief of one of the country's most powerful publishers. And then ask yourself, is Ms. Godoff alone, or are there hundreds or thousands of such culture police deployed across the country who, if they could not shut us up completely, at least systematically distort the substance of the debate about the future of America by omission and suppression?

The election of 2000 will be one more battle between the forces that either shaped or became admirers of the "youth movement" during the sixties and those who identified ourselves with Main Street America during those years. A large swath of the baby-boom generation sided with a new and radically dismissive vision of the American ideal that overtook elite culture in those years. But many of us—a majority in fact—recognized that the generation of our parents and elders had in fact achieved great things. The election of 2000 will, for the first time, be a contest between two baby boomers, one from each political camp. I intend to be the standard-bearer for those Americans of all ages who remain convinced that the values of the generation that fought and won World War II and then went on to build the country's enormous productive capacity are the values that should truly define this society.

American greatness is the product of a shared commitment to underlying values.

The founders of our country understood this. The letters from the leaders of the young republic brim with references to the importance of morality in American life. Ben Franklin spoke for the framers of the Constitution when he said that "[o]nly a virtuous people are capable of freedom." George Washington, in his farewell address, declared that "of all the dispositions and habits which lead to political prosperity, religion and morality are indispensable supports." His successor, John Adams, was even more direct: "Our Constitution was made only for a moral and religious people. It is wholly inadequate to the government of any other."

The founders appreciated that our Constitution depended upon a citizenry that was upright and self-disciplined because so much freedom was left with the people to run their daily lives. If the people grow attached to the wrong values, there is no authority to set them straight. That is the promise and the peril of the freedom we take for granted. James Madison, the primary drafter of the Constitution, summed it up perfectly: "We have staked the future of all our political institutions upon the capacity of each and all of us to control ourselves, to sustain ourselves according to the Ten Commandments."

Throughout this book, my aim is to clarify those values we hold dear and must defend. Broader values such as human life and the institutions of family and marriage I will take up later. For now, I want to highlight a few core values—also rightly called virtues—in order to make a point: Values do not exist in a vacuum. They thrive or perish in a democratic republic based on how much the people demand that those values be present in their leaders and on how much those leaders and others who mold public opinion are willing to set an example for the next generation.

Faith in God

Who is our sovereign? Of course it is God, not the state, not the government or any political movement. America is a God-fearing nation, and we must proceed from that basic premise.

This country was literally founded on faith in God. The Declaration of Independence stakes its claims on "the laws of Nature and of Nature's God" and argues not that men have secured liberty for themselves but that "their Creator" has endowed them with "certain unalienable rights." The country has flourished and survived because of that faith. I am a Christian, and I detailed my beliefs in *Standing Firm*. I am also persuaded that America is a uniquely blessed country, one with a mission of furthering and protecting freedom. I am not ashamed of my faith or of this country's collective faith. I am a pluralist as well, and I am proud that people of all different faiths have opted to make their home here, comfortable behind the great bulwark of religious liberty we have built over the centuries.

Ninety percent of Americans believe in God. Nearly 100 percent of the Congress of the United States does as well. It is an unequivocally good thing that we are a nation of believers and that many of us read, study, and try to conform our lives to the teachings of the Bible. It is time to end the scoffing at religion and especially at Christianity that goes on among the self-anointed elites in the media, the entertainment industry, and academia. It is remarkable that our media do not hesitate to publish or broadcast the most sordid details of sexual excess yet grow timid and defensive on matters of religion and faith.

People of deep religious conviction have been under a sustained assault for many years now. A good example of the thoroughness of this assault and the subtlety of its form came on February 1, 1993, on the front page of the *Washington Post*. In a story on "The Gospel Grapevine" came this segment:

> The gospel lobby evolved with the explosion of satellite and cable television, hitting its national political peak in the presidential election of Ronald Reagan in 1980.
>
> Unlike other powerful interests, it does not lavish campaign funds on candidates for Congress nor does it entertain them. The strength of the fundamentalist leaders lies in their flocks. Corporations pay public relations firms millions of dollars to contrive the kind of grass-roots response that [Jerry] Falwell or Pat Robertson can galvanize in a televised sermon. Their followers are largely poor, uneducated and easy to command.

An outraged readership obliged the *Post* to retract the statement the following day. The *Post*'s correction read: "An article yesterday characterized followers of television evangelists Jerry Falwell and Pat Robertson as 'largely poor, uneducated and easy to command.' There is no factual basis to that statement."

So why was this unfounded and bigoted statement published in the first place? Why didn't it set off alarms among the editors? They didn't know any better. And thus the episode at least allowed a glimpse of the real feelings of the opinion elite toward faith. This is an unfair and shameful mind-set, and a president can do much to reestablish the revered place of religious belief in our country without proposing a single rule, regulation, or law. We pose no risk to the separation of church and state by honoring the men and women who lead the faith communities in this country. Many of them are among my friends and longtime supporters. No intelligent observer who bothers to examine the issue can label the religious leadership of the United States or its followers as "largely poor, uneducated and easy to command." You cannot be "uneducated" and "easy to command" and yet found and lead the literally thousands of faith-based groups that successfully diagnose and treat the ills of modern America, from crisis pregnancies to the needs of AIDS patients to the care and rehabilitation of the homeless. The White House ought to highlight these leaders and the communities they captain. Whatever social ills afflict our neighborhoods, there are faith-based organizations doing their part to help alleviate the suffering. Often the only friend to the desperately poor and ill are these selfless groups. Moreover, such volunteers should be the very last people in this country the government should fear. America's volunteers should be encouraged at every turn.

INTEGRITY

It is difficult to say anything new about a virtue so old. Integrity has always meant a quality of uncompromising adherence to a clear standard of conduct. When parents ask their children to lead lives of integrity and honesty, they are seeking a commitment to many different values, but they are primarily asking them to act with regard to high ideals in a truthful, nonhypocritical way.

Especially in view of the past six years, the next president must be dedicated above all to restoring integrity and honesty to the Oval Office. This is an issue that transcends partisan differences: Jimmy Carter, Ronald Reagan, and George Bush all served honorably. It is time to reestablish this commitment to integrity as a precondition of presidential service. The country deserves no less.

We now find ourselves in a situation where the public is obliged to demand that candidates tell the truth about themselves. It's impossible to imagine President Eisenhower, say, or President Truman being accused of deceitfulness or a lack of credibility. The politics of their time was no less combative than today's, but they met their opponents and their arguments head-on and with a candor that many would find astonishing today.

Glibness is no substitute for integrity. America's schoolchildren need leaders they can look up to, not ones about whom explanations have to be given. We ask our children to be honest with us, to admit when they are wrong, and to acknowledge errors when they make them. These requests will be turned aside by children if they are ignored by those in high government office.

We must also realize that America can be called upon to face a crisis at a moment's notice. History teaches that we can move from a peacetime economy of great abundance to one of war or serious threat literally overnight. When such a challenge arrives—and it surely will—the public must have confidence in the integrity of its leaders. Without it, rallying the country, no matter how just the cause, will be difficult.

President Bush had such integrity, and as a result, when he summoned the vast power of the American military to confront Saddam Hussein, the American people trusted his decision to go to war, despite warnings that casualties could number in the tens of thousands.

When I was a young man, I learned firsthand that integrity often requires sacrifice of ambition. Back in 1972, my father, a staunch conservative, was offered the chairmanship of the Indiana Republican Party, a position of considerable visibility and some power. He would have greatly enjoyed the job.

But he turned it down. President Richard Nixon was up for reelection that year, and Dad, believing that Nixon had taken too many wrong turns on domestic policy, had decided to back the protest candidacy of conservative Ohio Congressman John Ashbrook. Dad knew that the people offering him the party chairmanship did so with the expectation that he would support Nixon. He could not honorably serve both them and his own conscience, so he declined.

A call to integrity is the internal compass we all carry. My father evaluated his own actions against that compass. So should we all.

Integrity cannot be measured, but it can be felt. It is the confidence that spoken words are true and not just that they are "not false." It is the confidence that national interest always trumps self-interest. It is, most of all, the confidence that the president is the people's servant, their agent, their representative.

RESPONSIBILITY

The Declaration of Independence represented a tremendous act of commitment. The patriots who drafted it were willing to take responsibility for their actions. To sign the Declaration was to sign a sort of contingent execution warrant. Had the Crown triumphed and the revolution been suppressed, they would have lost their property, their liberty, and almost certainly their lives.

Even in the face of such danger, however, they boldly called for revolution.

And they paid the price. Fifty-six patriots signed the Declaration. A monument in James River, Virginia, tells the rest of the story: "Nine signers died of wounds during the Revolutionary War. Five were captured or imprisoned; wives and children were killed, jailed, mistreated, or left penniless. Twelve signers' houses were burned to the ground. Seventeen lost everything they owned. No signer defected. Their honor, like their nation, remained intact."

The conduct of Dwight Eisenhower during World War II is another great example of personal responsibility in action. On the eve of the D-day invasion, with the risk of failure high, Eisenhower wrote out by hand a statement to be issued in the event the landings were turned back: "If any fault or blame attaches to the attempt, it is mine alone."

We need to remind ourselves of the simple definition of responsibility. It means the willingness to answer for our own conduct and our own obligations. It means choosing right over wrong. It means, finally, that our word is our bond.

Mistakes and grievous errors can and do occur. But accountability is required for errors of judgment and policy, and people who have developed an ethic of responsibility do not run from such mistakes. The particulars of error are not so much the issue as the need to establish an example for the country—especially for its young people—that maturity requires seeking and accepting responsibility. We cannot long endure as a democracy if we have leadership that never and nowhere accepts responsibility.

Better examples of corporate responsibility can help too. It makes little sense for corporate executives to reward themselves with huge salaries and bonuses that bear little relation to company performance. Last year, pay packages for the CEOs of America's 365 largest public companies increased by an average of 36 percent while those companies' profits fell by an average of 1.4 percent. More executives should follow the lead of Boeing executives Phil Condit and Henry Stonecipher, who decided to forego their 1998 bonuses in the wake of a disappointing year.

Responsibility is a value that parents grow hoarse encouraging in their children. We plead for responsibility, and we demand it. We do so because we know that responsible adults are those who can be trusted to live rightly and purposefully, to pull their oar.

All organizations depend upon the responsibility of their members. Even a few irresponsible people can cripple the effectiveness of a business, a school, or any kind of a sports team. When we speak of being "let down," chances are that someone has acted irresponsibly.

When we commit to acting responsibly, we commit to considering carefully our duties and obligations and to carrying out those duties and obligations. We commit without reservation to deliver the goods we promise, to make the effort we pledge, and to avoid looking for scapegoats if we fail.

As Winston Churchill observed, the price of greatness is responsibility. This is true for each of us as individuals and for the nation as a whole. This is a quality in eclipse in America's political leadership. We need it back.

COURAGE

Courage ranks first among the important virtues because without it all other virtues would perish in the face of opposition.

We have systematically devalued the word *courage*. We use it far too often in the context of mere politics. It is *never* courageous merely to risk a few votes, and we should stop equating everyday political maneuvering with courage. Politics sometimes does require the courage of conviction, such as when Henry Hyde and the House managers pushed for a verdict on President Clinton's perjury and obstruction of justice in the face of a unified front of pollsters and pundits warning them of electoral doom. Chairman Hyde and his colleagues put their principles ahead of their own political fortune—and that exemplified courage.

It takes real courage to patrol the streets of America's cities, especially when the police risk being outgunned and outnumbered.

It takes real courage to patrol the thirty-eighth parallel in a daily display of American purposefulness in Korea.

It takes real courage to walk through the metal detectors at the entrance of an urban high school every day to take up the task of teaching willing minds in an environment that is sometimes hostile and even dangerous for teachers.

Rosa Parks's refusal to give up her seat on that bus took real courage. Elie Wiesel's refusal to give up in the face of Nazi horror took real courage. Aleksandr Solzhenitsyn and his fellow dissidents from the communist gulags bore up only through courage. And the sacrifice of the protesters in Tiananmen Square is one that can be appropriately honored only if we do not devalue the word by confusing it with political posturing. Billy Graham put it well: "Courage is contagious. When a brave man takes a stand, the spines of others are stiffened."

COURTESY

Some may call it unrealistic to ask for a return to standards of public behavior that used to prevail throughout America. My eight years in the U.S. Senate and four in the House of Representatives taught me, as they teach many members of both parties, that political disagreements do not require that we be disagreeable. In fact, the opposite is true. Elaborate courtesy prevails at times of the most intense disagreement, an honoring of the commitment to civilized debate. Unfortunately, even this long-honored commitment has begun to fray.

America is now drenched in ratings-driven ranting and a frequent breaching of our commitment to civility. It is time to remind ourselves that courtesy is the oxygen of civil discourse, and representative democracy depends upon civil discourse. If we become accustomed to the vulgar and the coarse, the vulgar and the coarse will quickly overtake every good and decent thing. The common practice of courtesy is our first line of defense.

THRIFT

Parents worry that their children do not appreciate the virtue of thrift. Consumerism is so great that many young people think that to want something is to deserve it immediately.

Like courtesy, thrift may seem a quaint virtue. But think about it for a moment. Thrift is the exercise of self-restraint. It is a conservative wisdom handed down from generation to generation that "saving for a rainy day" is what you do first. The loss of that wisdom does more, however, than turn us and our children into binge shoppers. It also affects how we perceive the role of government.

If we put today's interests ahead of tomorrow's, our government will follow suit. If we do not view government as an institution of limited powers with an obligation to act wisely and frugally, the obvious course is to turn it into one massive spending machine with a program for every interest group. In other words, thrift and big government cannot permanently co-exist.

The hard work of generations past built up today's great infrastructure. But we need the same spirit of self-sacrifice and saving they displayed if we are to leave our children and grandchildren the same kind of opportunity we have enjoyed. We can choose to consume everything we have built and everything we have inherited. But we would be the first generation of Americans to do so. I cannot believe we will allow ourselves to squander this inheritance like the prodigal son.

The virtue of thrift is closely connected to the virtue of patience, and we must commit ourselves to long-term prosperity, both as individuals and as a nation. When big government takes more of our money than is really necessary, it takes away our freedom to make choices we can make more wisely than any bureaucrat can. Punishing thrift—for example, through inheritance taxes—is simply wrong.

VALUES DO MATTER MOST

I'm often asked by people who consider themselves economic conservatives—those who believe passionately in free markets and free enterprise—why I place so much emphasis on the importance of values. I answer that the free market system is based on trust. Billions of economic transactions occur every day, and each comes down to an agreement between two sides, freely made and freely carried out. Sellers expect to receive payment; buyers expect to get what they paid for. Employers expect employees to be honest, hardworking, and drug-free. Workers expect to be paid on schedule. Parents expect childcare workers to be conscientious. Retirees expect their pensions to be administered honestly. As James Q. Wilson phrased it, "The public interest depends on private virtue."

In short, regardless of whether one's primary interest is in economic issues or in social issues, we all have a stake in the debate on values. Without them, our economy will no longer lead the world. And our country will evolve to a different sort of government—one that controls us because we're no longer able to control ourselves.

Middle-class values are broadly based and widely admired across America. But they do have their mockers and indeed their enemies. Defending middle-class values is not always pleasant. In our day, it requires thick skin. But these values are certainly worth fighting for, not only because they represent what's best about America, but because they are the keys to our future freedom and prosperity.

3

What the Sixties Did

I NCREDIBLE as it may seem, we continue to be in the midst of debates begun in the sixties. Today, the boomers have become middle-aged. Some of them have ascended to positions of power and influence in government and media, and they insist that the issues they raised in the sixties are still open. Some of the "Me Generation" people now occupy positions that allow them to influence public opinion, and some of them continue to peddle nostalgia for their years of self-indulgence. We continue to pay a price for the excesses of the crowd that preached free drugs, free love, free lunch, and freedom from responsibility.

The sixties began in the high purpose and drama of the civil rights movement. But that noble effort was soon overshadowed by excesses wholly unrelated to the struggle for civil rights. The social upheavals triggered by the first large-scale infusion of drugs into our culture and the enormous human toll of the Vietnam War quickly overwhelmed the country, and a long period of cultural chaos followed. The fear generated by riots and protests opened deep divisions in the country. I was a student at DePauw when Dr. Martin Luther King Jr. was murdered, and I shared in the sadness and dismay that swept the country. Bobby Kennedy was in Indianapolis that night, and my respect for him soared as he bravely walked the streets, urging calm. Kennedy himself was assassinated just two months later on the night he won the California presidential primary. It is hard to convey to the youth of today the turmoil of that era, but three decades later the conflicts that erupted then continue to affect our politics.

The radical youth of the sixties made many serious mistakes, both in their lifestyles and in their political choices. As the files of the Soviet Union have become available, these one-time protestors have had to come to grips with the reality of the evils of the communism they once apologized for. As drugs have claimed hundreds of thousands of lives and poisoned millions more, the "new morality" of the sixties is easily recognized today as the wedge that pried open the country to the routine use of drugs. Finally, the rejection of traditional sexual morality that spread almost overnight in those turbulent years robbed and continues to rob an army of children of the chance to live in two-parent households, even as it unleashed a plague of sexually transmitted diseases from herpes to AIDS to hepatitis B.

The wreckage of the sixties is so massive that many members of that generation refuse to confront it fairly.

The sixties radicals were never remotely as numerous as their publicity suggested. But they were a privileged group, and that privilege has now put them into positions of extraordinary influence from which they continue to combat traditional values. These debates ought to have ended long ago, but those who attacked the middle class and its values have too much invested in the misbegotten culture of their youth to own up to their enormous errors of judgment. Instead they now use their influence—influence far disproportionate to their numbers—to go on savaging the same values that they were attacking three decades ago.

There are in America various groups of people enjoying almost breathtaking privilege, each one of which is dominated by individuals who got the major issues of the sixties wrong. The members of these groups generally enjoy enormous wealth and virtually unassailable professional security. They answer either to no one (in the case of federal judges and tenured university faculty) or to only a few like-minded people (in the case of producers, directors, and senior editors). A numbing near-uniformity of opinion and taste has settled over these specially privileged groups. Their collective mind-set is significantly to the left of the political center in this country, and that simple fact has tilted the country's culture in a direction that is counter to middle-class values.

There is, of course, no vast, left-wing conspiracy, just like there is no vast, right-wing conspiracy. But there is a class of people who collectively drive the culture of the United States. Journalist and author Michael Lind calls it "the overclass." Others call it the "opinion elite." I call it the *new aristocracy.* I use the term purposefully, because like the English aristocracy, this American aristocracy does not depend for its position on popular consent.

The elite news media, the Hollywood crowd, the tenured faculty of elite institutions of higher education, the federal judiciary, and the radical feminist movement together make up this new class. Their numbers are small, but their collective influence is staggering.

THE OPINION ELITE

The members of the new aristocracy are the cultural mapmakers of the country. They try to design the roads along which we will all have to travel. They post the signs. They publish the guidebooks. They exhort, they cajole, and they reward as well as punish. They want to steer every wheel.

The good news is that, despite the collective power of the opinion elite, the American electorate remains remarkably steady on its own old and tested routes. Public officials get reminded of this on occasion.

Nevertheless, bit by bit the elite culture has been wearing away at the old habits of mind. For politicians, very few things are as seductive as the temptation to trim one's positions in order to be toasted by the Beltway media giants and their cousins in New York. Unfortunately, as former *National Review* editor John O'Sullivan has noted, many Republicans have done just that and now "speak the elite's languages as the Democrats do, honor and obey the basic tenets of orthodox feminism, [and] are no more hemmed in by traditional family structure."

One of the most remarkable pieces of research on media attitudes was a 1996 Roper Center survey of the voting preferences of Washington-based reporters. Only 7 percent said they had voted for George Bush in 1992. The poll also revealed that 61 percent of the reporters labeled themselves as "moderate to liberal," and only 9 percent called themselves "moderate to conservative." Remember that in 1992 Bill Clinton was elected with only 43 percent of the votes cast. But a full 89 percent of those reporters voted for him. That kind of disconnect between the nation's opinions and the opinion of its capital reporters cannot but be reflected in the coverage of news and the interpretation of past events.

When Ted Turner's "historians" at CNN turned their attention to the Cold War, they repeatedly wandered, as columnist Charles

Krauthammer put it, "beyond mere moral equivalence to cheap anti-Americanism." CNN's revisionist historians explain that Joseph Stalin was "forced" to form the Soviet bloc in response to American and Western assertiveness and that the announcement of the Truman Doctrine was the "official declaration of the Cold War." The era of the 1950s, viewers are told, brought two equivalent horrors: Hollywood blacklists and Soviet gulags; never mind that the gulags were responsible for millions of deaths. As for the end of the Cold War, wrote Gabriel Schoenfeld in *Commentary*, the CNN series "succeed[ed] in doing the impossible: giving credit to Moscow for terminating the conflict and blaming Washington for attempting to extend it." This twenty-four-part miniseries proved again and again that no triumph of freedom is ever itself free from being distorted and belittled by the aging campus radicals who learned in the sixties that America was an "oppressor."

On issue after issue, it has become routine for elite journalists and filmmakers to reinforce the opinions of liberal Democratic leaders. A study recently published by the Yale University Press found that journalists, not surprisingly, tend to share a "cluster of attitudes that includes suspicion of business and the military and support for feminism, affirmative action, gay rights, and abortion rights." On that last issue, there is not a single major news anchor or managing editor who is known to value the life of the unborn over a "woman's right to choose." That doesn't reflect opinion in America, but it is the way of the media.

HOLLYWOOD

In the minds of many, my *Murphy Brown* speech was an attack on Hollywood. Actually it was not an "attack" but a critique of a particular kind of entertainment—the trivialization of crucial subjects. The images, themes, and points of view conveyed by the entertainment industry do have real world impact. They affect our lives and souls, sometimes dramatically, sometimes subtly.

To those who doubt this proposition, I ask, why do advertisers spend a million dollars for a minute of commercial time during the Super Bowl? Ads work because behavior is influenced by the messages we receive over and over again, even when our critical thinking is on full alert.

Leftists admit this when it suits their ideology. Feminists, for example, have routinely complained that roles for "strong leading women" are rare and that weak women in television and movie dramas do a disservice to equality. When Al Gore praised the television series *Ellen* for, in his word, "forcing" Americans to view a positive portrayal of a lesbian relationship, he too was confirming my essential point: The entertainment industry—a "Hollywood" that is much bigger than the movie and television industry alone— has a great deal of influence on the culture.

When Ellen DeGeneres "came out" on television, I received a call from Diane Sawyer, who wanted to know what I thought. I declined comment on Ms. DeGeneres's personal life, but I did note that if Hollywood really wanted to act courageously, it would premier a show starring and favorably portraying any female who was pro-life and Christian.

In a television interview, Diane Sawyer asked Ms. DeGeneres about my comment. After a pause, she agreed. And so would all honest observers of the small screen.

The values that the entertainment industry brings to the creation of its product are vastly different from those of the middle class. Hollywood's version of reality usually favors the extremely liberal. In his wonderful book *Hollywood vs. America*, Michael Medved has detailed the particulars, and I should not have to repeat his argument for fair-minded people to recognize that the fight to preserve middle-class values is frequently in opposition to the Hollywood version of reality. A recent study by Wade Horn's National Fatherhood Initiative found that only 15 out of 102 prime-time TV shows depicted fathers as regular, central characters. An analysis conducted by the Office of National Drug Control Policy found that 81 percent of references to drug use made in popular songs and 52 percent of those made in movies omitted mention of any negative consequences.

Wouldn't it be refreshing to see Hollywood produce entertainment that at least half of the time depicts marriages as worth saving, families as worth having, and flags as worth waving? If this powerful art form were ever to get its moral bearings, it could become a tremendous booster of cultural renewal and not the obstacle to middle-class values that it too often is. Moreover, the industry itself would be better off: A number of studies have proved that G-rated, family-oriented films are far more profitable than movies containing graphic sex and violence.

THE FACULTY LOUNGE

It is a good thing that the faculties of the elite universities of the United States do not have immediate power. The collective ideological disposition of this group is firmly anchored to the left of Hollywood, which is itself to the left of the opinion elite.

The septic shock that hit the American universities in the late sixties and early seventies was an illness with lasting effects that are now nearly untreatable due to the educational rigor mortis called tenure. Self-congratulation over faculty "diversity" often masks a rigid ideological conformity: white liberals, black liberals, male liberals, female liberals, old liberals, and young liberals. One conservative professor told me recently that his job interview had involved more questions about his political views than about his scholarly interests. A tenured faculty member pointedly asked, "On this campus, our values are very liberal; what makes you think you will fit in here?"

A concise summary of the left's agenda is easiest to find in the course catalogs of America's colleges. Indeed, every Ivy League college with the exception of Princeton now offers more courses in "women's studies" than in economics. Dartmouth College initially prohibited the free distribution of copies of *Mere Christianity* by C. S. Lewis after a dean determined that the book could be considered offensive. Recently, I read an account of a conference on pornography put on by California State University at Northridge. Sadly, I was not surprised to see taxpayer dollars going into a "conference" at which one room was devoted to a film festival of X-rated porn. The pseudointellectual appeal of this sort of exercise is by now so familiar that it occasioned no outrage or protest. Just another day at your friendly local university.

Most voters discount the politics of America's professors. But this nonchalance about what the professors are up to is troubling, because it overlooks that they are the *teachers*. Princeton has given a distinguished chair in bioethics to a philosopher who, according to the *New York Times*, believes that "a newborn has no greater right to life than any other being of comparable rationality and capacity for emotion, including pigs, cows, and dogs."

We not only recognize college professors as people who *can* mold minds, we *ask* and *expect* them to do so! The middle class is subsidizing this collegiate assault on their own values—and knowingly acquiescing. Why?

RULERS IN ROBES

More than a century and a half ago, Alexis de Tocqueville wrote in *Democracy in America* that there "is hardly a political question in the United States which does not sooner or later turn into a judicial one." But the situation today is far worse than Tocqueville could ever have imagined. As Sen. Jeff Sessions of Alabama has remarked, "The federal courts have usurped one political issue after another: Abortion, homosexual rights, school busing, racial preferences, term limits, [and] criminal procedure" with disastrous consequences. Abortion, of course, is the most prominent of these; as legal scholar Mary Ann Glendon has noted, by seizing control of the issue, the unelected federal judiciary for twenty years imposed on America the most radical abortion policy in the industrialized world, with the possible exception of the People's Republic of China. Citizens vote, but judges now rule.

Judges who impose their own policy preferences through court order are not being faithful to their duty under the Constitution. It is absolutely critical that the next round of appointees to the Supreme Court and the lower federal courts be men and women who will act as impartial interpreters of the law, not as the self-anointed agents of the modern liberal agenda.

RADICAL FEMINISTS

No single group has more pervasive influence on the media elite than do radical feminists. This group of lobbyists and politicians represents a very small slice of the American electorate, but they regularly appear on television to speak on behalf of the nation's women. The radical feminist agenda is not principally about opening opportunities for women. Instead, as writer Jennifer Robak Moore notes, modern feminism is the "ideological veil for a political special interest group."

Nor, as the Clinton scandals made clear, is the agenda of the National Organization for Women, the Fund for a Feminist Majority, Emily's List, and the National Abortion Rights Action League about protecting women in the workplace—just ask Paula Jones, Kathleen Willey, or Juanita Broaddrick. When Barbra Streisand and Eleanor Smeal give speeches, you can be sure they won't be giving the president a lecture on work environments that are hostile toward women.

Rather, the radical feminists are attempting to homogenize American women into a single ideological mold. "The salient characteristic of contemporary feminism," observed Carolyn Graglia in *Domestic Tranquility*, "is that it belittles and seeks to undermine a woman's traditional role as wife and mother." Why else would early leaders of the feminist movement like Betty Friedan intentionally condemn housewives as "parasites" and Gloria Steinem dismiss homemakers as "dependent creatures who are still children"?

I have no objection to radical feminists advocating the merits of their position; that's what free debate is all about. But they do not speak for America's women. They only speak for America's liberals.

Republicans must understand that the gender gap is not the product of feminist opposition. They should not be cowed by these radicals from asserting principled arguments for protecting the unborn and promoting teenage sexual abstinence. This self-anointed elite has never and *will* never vote GOP. Most women want from their government the same things that men want: good neighborhood schools, safe streets, lower taxes, a healthy economy, a clean environment, and honesty in the White House.

CONGRESS

You'll notice that I don't include the U.S. Congress as part of the new aristocracy. This is because an elected body representing the two major political parties and the full range of differing opinions presents a different type of problem: Congress suffers from an institutional tendency to be out of touch with the voters. After a few terms in office it is easy to succumb to the perks and privileges of power. In recent decades, incumbent reelection rates have never fallen below 85 percent; for members who have served more than six years, the reelection rate is 99 percent. The framers of the Constitution never intended for members of Congress to serve for twenty, thirty, or forty years; rather, they envisioned congressional service as a temporary honor, following which a member would return to his home district or state. That is why, as my very first act as a member of Congress in 1977, I introduced legislation to limit congressional terms. Nothing since then has changed my view that it is time to revive the framers' vision and require members of Congress to go back home to live under the laws they've been passing for the rest of us.

ANSWERING THE ARISTOCRACY

The sources of the attack on middle-class values are many and powerful. But they are not invulnerable, and they can be beaten. We just have to remember that the cultural divide did not develop overnight, and it cannot be healed overnight.

But a change in course *must* occur. That is, the defenders of traditional values must begin to go on the offensive in a consistent, purposeful fashion. There have been some impressive recent efforts: the advent of the *Weekly Standard,* for instance. Folks like Bill Bennett, Pat Robertson, Cal Thomas, Mona Charen, Thomas Sowell, Linda Chavez, Tony Snow, Michael Medved, and a number of others are carrying the flag of common sense into the mainstream media. And institutions like Hillsdale College and a growing network of denominational colleges and universities (including the newly formed Ave Maria School of Law, a Catholic institution endowed by Domino's Pizza founder Tom Monaghan) are training a new generation of leaders.

But the electorate must have before it a group of candidates courageous enough to speak these very obvious truths even though they and their message will be slandered and distorted. Only when those speeches are made and the candidates who make them are elected will public policy move enthusiastically back to the center.

As a matter of strategy, it is important to identify and appoint cultural critics of ability and intellect to the key posts of secretary of education and chairmen of the National Endowments for the Humanities and the Arts, so long as these posts exist. These men and women would do the indispensable work of engaging the new aristocracy and exposing the emptiness of its rhetoric and its posturing. For too long conservatives have been willing to tolerate the awful imbalance in access to the means of communicating with the American people. But we can and must talk our way back to center stage.

The collective contempt of the cultural elites for middle-class values and aspirations does have a dispiriting effect on the country. The bewilderment at vulgar entertainment, or journalistic bias, or faculty or judicial extremism can lead to a feeling of hopelessness or, even worse, to self-pity. Too many conservatives forget that the most successful American conservative of this century, Ronald Reagan, relied on sheer optimism no matter how daunting the challenge. And the most important Englishman of this century, Winston Churchill, relied on the blunt direction "Never, never, never, never give up!" It is no accident that both of these great men rejected bitterness and cynicism. Each of them endured a lot of sneering. Of Ronald Reagan's entry into the 1980 presidential race, Meg Greenfield of the *Washington Post* wrote, "It was the wisdom of the other contenders and of most Republican Party leaders too, not to mention of practically everyone in Democratic politics, that Reagan was: too old, too extreme, too marginal and not nearly smart enough to win the nomination. The Democrats, in fact, when they weren't chortling about him, were fervently hoping he would be the nominee."

Both Reagan and Churchill had their low political moments— Reagan's defeat when he sought the GOP nomination in 1976 and Churchill's "wilderness years" in the thirties. But even when it appeared as though both had been permanently exiled from leadership, both refused to give in to despair or to walk away from the crucial debate of the day. Churchill remained the vigilant if lonely herald of the dark news in Europe. Reagan, too, was vigilant in his opposition to both the Soviet Union and our country's swelling government. Both men's fidelity to principle in the face of disdain and dismissal did much to rally the vast portion of their countrymen to the challenges that eventually arrived.

Furthermore, both did so with humor and grace. Neither allowed his deep-seated convictions to poison his relations with even his greatest domestic political enemies. And conservatives today similarly cannot allow their sense of powerlessness over the culture to develop into a resigned bitterness. We must fight back, and we must prevail.

American culture can and will be transformed by a public that is slowly awakening to the damage done to our system of values. This is the area in which the president's greatest impact comes through the appointments he makes and the message he delivers from the famed bully pulpit.

It is time to convene a White House conference on intellectual diversity in American universities. The National Association of Scholars has long waged a battle to open modern college faculties to the diversity of opinion in America. Too often conservative scholars are shut out of the best appointments and the prestigious grants. While a president can do little to affect the actual hiring decisions made by faculties that are far removed from the center of American public opinion, he can commit the resources necessary to explore fully and expose to the public the depth of ideological prejudice now present in our higher education system.

Second, the textbooks from which our elementary and high school students learn are crucial in transmitting more than equations and dates, geography and the periodic table. They incorporate and transmit values as well, and frequently those values are not the values of honest, hardworking, middle-class Americans. While this problem is most easily seen in the health and sex education curricula, other things—for instance, the battles over the national education standards that have raged during the Clinton-Gore years—testify to the endemic bias among education elites. My sister-in-law has served on the Textbook Commission of Tennessee, and I have been appalled at many of the textbooks that she and her colleagues evaluate and that are used in our nation's public schools.

Republicans hold thirty-one governorships, including those in eight of the ten largest states. These governors, along with conservative intellectuals—and certain courageous, independent Democrats who are willing to risk the wrath of powerful teachers unions—should band together to force change. I hope to see this group produce a "best of" list covering textbooks. I hope the list would be long, but if only a handful of textbooks were to qualify, then only a few would be recommended. And this list would need to be publicized coast to coast.

Initiatives like the conference on intellectual diversity and the effort to evaluate textbooks will predictably bring forth howls of protest from the left. And when they do, conservatives will need to remember Ronald Reagan's great response to Jimmy Carter: "There you go again." In that good-humored but dismissive phrase resides the secret to the conservative renaissance: an amused bewilderment at how some people will never give up deploying more rhetoric in their efforts to defeat mainstream common sense. If conservatives stay the course in declaring and defending the values the country embodies, the radicals' fear-mongering will not dent our public support.

Many among the new aristocracy are willing to practice the "politics of personal destruction" even as they denounce it. Conservatives need to be mindful of this fury on the left and never underestimate its vehemence. But our party and its leaders must refuse to sink to a level where politics depends more upon attack ads, scurrilous leaks, and upside-down spin than it does upon the ideas that made the country great.

4

The Hot Buttons

SOME ISSUES seem always to divide rather than to unite our nation. When our bedrock values compel us to take a certain policy stand, attempts at compromise are bound to fail. When this happens within a family, we can agree not to discuss certain matters over the dinner table and thereby keep peace in the household. When this happens within the nation, however, we must discuss the issues, but with civility and mutual respect.

A president is supposed to lead those discussions, not hide from them. That is why, in this chapter, I lay out my views on some of the most controversial issues in contemporary politics.

LIFE IS WORTH FIGHTING FOR

The ultimate test of leadership is the willingness to make decisions without regard to polls, politics, or pressure. As our country endeavors to reverse the social decline of the last quarter-century, one of the core values we must rediscover is respect for the sanctity of human life.

Asserting that value can be difficult and divisive. But all that is best in the American character and conscience calls us to pursue it. The decisions we face are hard ones, but they become especially difficult only when we attempt to straddle them.

Let's get this straight: Republicans do not lose elections by sincerely standing for life. They do not court defeat by forthrightly defending children before birth and elderly patients at the end of life. Ronald Reagan knew our pro-life platform was right. The American voter respects candidates who put honest principle ahead of other considerations.

Since my first year in Congress in 1977, when I cosponsored a human life amendment, I have consistently stood for the sanctity of human life. I believe that ending an innocent life can be justified only when necessary to save another life. I stand for these principles, not for political advantage, but because the destruction of innocent human beings transgresses what Ronald Reagan called, in the title of his book, *The Conscience of the Nation*.

We need to make our case more effectively and bring to our side those who are not totally wedded to the abortion-on-demand agenda. But the times call for more than rhetoric.

Our goal should be to save every child, for who is to say which tiny boys and girls are expendable because of a handicap, or gender, or inconvenience? But if this is a journey of a thousand miles—or a hundred million hearts—it will begin, and proceed, one step at a time.

That first step, clearly, should be a ban on the barbaric practice of partial-birth abortion. Destroying a near- or full-term baby is indefensible.

A sound second step, already introduced in Congress by

Rep. Ileana Ros-Lehtinen of Florida and Sen. Spence Abraham of Michigan, is the Child Custody Act. Its enactment would crack down on the abuse of young girls by adults who get around state parental notification laws by taking a minor to an out-of-state abortion clinic.

Another step that can be taken right away is full enforcement of state and federal laws against statutory rape. A shocking percentage of teen pregnancies and teen abortions result from statutory rape—the sexual exploitation of teens by adults. In recent decades, it's been considered rather old-fashioned to object to that conduct, and prosecution for statutory rape has become rare. That must change. Every rapist should be prosecuted to the full extent of the law.

Meanwhile, we should make sure that no federal program promotes abortion in any way. That especially includes Title X of the Public Health Service Act, an originally well-intentioned family-planning program that has become, instead, an enormous annual subsidy to the abortion industry—targeting teens without any requirement for parental consent.

We should also enhance penalties for crimes of violence when they are committed against a pregnant woman, thereby extending the protections of the law to the unborn baby. When a pregnant woman is assaulted or abused, she should have legal recourse against the damage done both to her and to her child.

I also believe it is time for a national effort to ensure that mothers with problem pregnancies have the support they need for themselves and their babies. In addition, we should do more to ensure that the many families who wish to adopt children can do so, and we should do everything we can to support and encourage the thousands of crisis pregnancy centers across the nation.

This, then, is my commitment: to speak and to act in defense of human life, from its earliest beginning to its final moments, with both determination and patience and, most of all, with the hopeful spirit that, over time, can touch hearts and change minds to care for the least of our brethren.

Rolling Back the Sexual Revolution

America, as I have said, has paid a heavy price for the excesses of the sixties. "If it feels good, do it," we were told. With that attitude, should we be surprised that one-third of our children are now being born in homes without fathers? Or that sexually transmitted diseases are reaching epidemic proportion? Or that divorce rates skyrocketed?

I am convinced that every issue involving sexual behavior and ethics is best understood as an issue of defending marriage and the family. I unequivocally support policies that promote and strengthen marriage and families. I unequivocally oppose policies that undermine those precious institutions.

I oppose "gay marriage," for example, because marriage ought to be a lifelong union of a man and woman. Such a union is a Judeo-Christian absolute and, as such, a hallmark of Western civilization. We must defend the special place that marriage holds in our private lives and in our civilization as a whole by resisting all attempts to equate same-sex relationships with marriage. It is in our country's best interest to help promote marriage and stable families presided over by both a mother and a father. As we are learning at great cost, when families fail, society suffers.

Finally, I reject additional "orientation"-specific rights. All Americans, including homosexuals, enjoy equal rights before the law, and I will vigorously defend every individual's right to equal and fair treatment. I will not support special rights for a few.

On the issue of sex education, we've seen a good deal of willful blindness to facts and common sense. So-called comprehensive sex education, with its blatant emphasis on the sex act rather than on values, is another attack on marriage and the family. As Barbara

Dafoe Whitehead reported in *The Atlantic* in 1994, this educational fraud, now mandated by nearly twenty states, is "a gumbo of ideas based on no known field of knowledge." Parents are right to be concerned about nonstop sex education from kindergarten through high school; after all, as Thomas Sowell observed, "It could not possibly take that much time to teach the basic biological or medical information about sex."

Sex education should—but usually doesn't—stress abstinence. Instead, current sex education programs stress the use of condoms. Condoms do not ensure protection against AIDS and should never be distributed in schools. Handing out condoms to children is analogous to offering classes on how best to drive drunk. Yet it happens routinely in spite of parents' wishes.

The bitter harvest of the sexual revolution is now so obvious that only the ideologically blinded can deny it. The statistics on sexually transmitted diseases are startling. Each year in the United States twelve million *new* cases of STDs are reported. Of these, three hundred thousand are teenagers—equaling a new case every three minutes. Many of these diseases are not inconsequential, as the awful carnage of AIDS has proved.

Hard-core liberals are reluctant to admit that the lifestyle revolution they launched in the sixties has become so destructive of human happiness. But the American people now understand clearly the costs of permissiveness, and they are resolved to reverse this downward spiral.

GUNS

Two friends, walking through a rough neighborhood after dark, are confronted by a dozen or so men who, without provocation, harass and begin to chase them. The friends run, having no doubt that if caught they will be badly beaten, perhaps even killed. One of the pursued suddenly turns and pulls out a handgun. End of confrontation. The leader of the gang then "demands officiously: 'Have you got a permit for that?'"

This story, related by Jonathan Rauch of the *National Journal*, captures the essence of the gun debate in America: Law-abiding citizens fear for their lives, and criminals become moralists.

I have always been a defender of the Second Amendment, which guarantees our right to keep and bear arms. I don't intend to canvass the full range of controversies that surround the gun issue but instead wish to make one point: Just about every gun-control proposal put foward—even when cast in terms of depriving criminals of weapons—is in fact directed at law-abiding citizens. That emphasis is exactly backward. It is estimated that only 7 percent of guns used by criminals were obtained legally.

University of Chicago scholar John R. Lott Jr. has now convincingly documented that crime drops when citizens are allowed to carry concealed weapons. His research proves that guns have effectively served their self-defense role in millions of incidents annually. Most important among these is the eye-opening Department of Justice report that the probability of serious injury from an attack is 2.5 times greater for women offering no resistance than for women resisting with a gun.

I grew up in Indiana and Arizona, two states where firearms and especially rifles and shotguns are commonplace. As a pre-teen, I was a graduate of the National Rifle Association's safety school. I have always enjoyed hunting. The ready availability of weapons in my home and in the homes of my friends did not change our personalities. We had all been taught responsible gun use and ownership. We had been taught values that precluded the irresponsible and evil use of weapons.

The tragedies of mass shootings shock us all. But I find it irrational that we so readily accept gun control as the answer to the diseased culture that produces kids who are willing to gun down their schoolmates and teachers. Values matter most. We must focus on parental responsibility and the need to give all our children a firm spiritual foundation. And we must confront an entertainment culture that produces an endless stream of computer games, movies, television shows, books, plays, and music that glorify mayhem and damage the soul.

Instant background checks before the purchase of a weapon are of course important and should continue. And we must increase the punishment for anyone using or even carrying a gun during the commission of a crime. But we have to recognize that criminals, by definition, will continue to acquire guns illegally and that police cannot protect everyone at all times. Many citizens choose to protect themselves. I will not allow the federal government to interfere with that protection.

I doubt if one in ten members of the media elite owns a weapon. They can afford exclusive neighborhoods and alarm systems to insulate them from the dangers facing many Americans. But elite distance from and disdain for the need for personal security cannot be allowed to distort the broad consensus that law-abiding citizens should determine for themselves what makes them safer.

ONE STRIKE AND YOU'RE OUT

Our criminal justice system—which once was a source of pride—now often divides and infuriates us. From the O. J. Simpson trial, to the Clinton investigation, to the demagogues who cry out for "hate crime" laws, we are witnessing cultural and political conflicts played out in a system that ought to be impartial and above reproach—a system in which every citizen can have complete confidence that justice will prevail.

Unfortunately, the criminal justice system does not always reflect our primary goals to provide justice to victims and to protect our people, particularly the most vulnerable. Regrettably, this focus is often lost. Thus, we endure a system that still allows convicted murderers to elude their capital punishment sentences for years on end. We allow young predators—as vicious as any adult—the escape hatch of a juvenile crime system that was designed for much less violent offenses in a much less violent culture. And, in another manifestation of the intellectual fads of the sixties, we pay more attention to the "rights" of criminals than to the rights of victims.

To sketch out every anticrime measure that is necessary would take an entire book in itself. But I do want to make one point very clear: Some crimes are so heinous and so likely to be repeated that any thought of "rehabilitation" must give way to common sense. Rapists and child molesters simply cannot be given the opportunity to repeat their atrocities. While federal law reaches relatively few cases of rape and molestation because they are primarily state-law issues, I do intend to set an example for the states on these issues.

Anyone guilty of aggravated rape or of child molestation should go to prison and never emerge. The victims of these crimes deserve nothing less than such a commitment.

5

Religion and Politics

COMMENTATORS are constantly singling out the "religious right" as a source of trouble for the Republican Party. They warn us that the religious right is a millstone around our collective neck, dragging us down to electoral disaster. But just who or what this fabled religious right composes, the opinion class is never precise about. If there is such a group as the religious right, then logically, I suppose, there must also be a pagan left.

THE LEGACY OF RELIGION IN AMERICA

Whenever the subject turns to religion and politics, people should be reminded of religion's historic pedigree in American society, beginning with the Massachusetts Bay Colony. A strong religious tradition inspired the patriots who called upon "the Laws of Nature and of Nature's God" to explain their right to independence from England. The generation of the founding fathers represented the first intermingling of religion and American politics.

The next spiritual wave was led by those who demanded an end to slavery. Many abolitionists were evangelical Protestants who had been swept into the antislavery movement by the Second Great Awakening. Harriet Beecher Stowe's *Uncle Tom's Cabin* was a wake-up call to the religious conscience of the country. "Mrs. Stowe (or perhaps God)," wrote Civil War historian James McPherson, "rebuked the whole nation for the sin of slavery. She aimed the novel at the evangelical conscience of the North. And she hit her mark."

A third legacy of religion in politics, though rarely discussed, is the right of women to vote. Religious zeal provided the inspiration for many leaders of the women's suffrage movement. Similarly, the fourth great marker of religion in politics—the civil rights movement of the early sixties—was born in black churches and drew its courage from a bedrock faith in God's justice.

Time and time again, religion has infused political movements in America. Until recently the church has been welcomed, but in recent years it has been libeled instead.

My friend Chuck Colson has commented that the "isms" of this century—communism, socialism, nazism, fascism, humanism, scientism, and liberalism—have all exhausted themselves. He points in agreement to Pope John Paul II's declaration that the year 2000 will usher in "a springtime of Christianity." Perhaps another "awakening" has begun, one in which men and women recognize that the secular world cannot provide genuine fulfillment. The gods of the sixties—total choice, no limits—may shortly be overthrown by the God who has been the center of American life for almost four centuries.

Many religious conservatives come to politics only after they have fed the poor in a thousand food banks, given shelter to the homeless in hundreds of housing construction efforts, comforted the abused and neglected in women and children's shelters across the country, and cared for the sick in hospices and hospitals that are explicitly faith-based. This is hardly the behavior of "radicals," as the left has labeled them.

If these grace-directed people and institutions suddenly vanished from our country, the social safety net would collapse immediately.

People of faith once again have begun to understand that their faith requires them to act as responsible citizens and become involved in public affairs. The involvement of religious people in the political process is an affirmation of the freedom guaranteed by the Bill of Rights, not a violation of it.

Ultraliberal groups like People for the American Way would have us believe that religious conservatives want to establish a theocracy. But examine the agenda of the Christian Coalition and you will be surprised to see a set of mainstream, common-sense proposals. Recently I reread the Christian Coalition's 1996 "Contract with the American Family." This document includes a call to restore the standard tax deduction for children to its inflation-adjusted 1946 value of eight thousand to ten thousand dollars per dependent child. It calls for privatization of the National Endowments for the Humanities and the Arts, the Corporation for Public Broadcasting, and the Legal Services Corporation, and it concludes with a demand for crime-victim restitution. Such an agenda is shocking only to the fringe of the Democratic Party.

A final but very important note. The tragic resort to violence by what is truly the lunatic fringe has resulted in accusations against the entire community of religious conservatives. This is plain slander. Ideological fanatics on both political extremes have killed doctors and burned buildings to the ground. They have blown up abortion clinics, and they have assaulted testing laboratories. They have used mail bombs and pipe bombs to kill people in the name of environmental extremism, and they have attacked defenseless men and women on the basis of race and sexual orientation. All such violence is evil. Those who blur the lines that separate ideological passion from ideological extremism only widen the divide that already threatens America.

The demonization of politics has been almost exclusively a one-sided affair. When the left attacked in sequence Robert Bork, Clarence Thomas, and Ken Starr, it did so only to avoid the need to grapple with these men's well-reasoned constitutional vision and sincerely held beliefs. Never was "the politics of personal destruction" more repugnant than when it was launched against Clarence Thomas, an honorable and talented man of principle. Thomas was attacked because he is a black conservative; the left organized the attacks against him because Thomas was, plain and simple, a threat to their agenda.

Fortunately, like Clarence Thomas, religious conservatives are men and women of courage who will not be deterred. Like their early forebears in the Revolutionary and Civil Wars and in the suffrage and civil rights movements, they too will overcome.

6

Faith-Based Organizations

FOR MOST of the postwar years, Americans stood by and watched as various indices of social ills climbed higher and higher. Even the most casual review of the past half-century yields startling statistics:

- Twice as many Americans were murdered in the United States from 1990 to 1994 as were killed in the Vietnam War.
- In 1950, eighty-eight out of one hundred children were born into an intact family. Today, only sixty out of one hundred children enter life with that same stability.
- Nearly 80 percent of children born in some urban areas are born into single-parent families.

The downward spiral is staggering and is little relieved by a recent decline in crime rates and a small drop in the number of abortions. Yes, there *is* good news. Republican-led efforts to toughen sentencing laws through "three strikes" reforms, for instance, have helped. And the Republican Congress passed and obliged Bill Clinton to sign a tough welfare-reform bill that promotes work and personal responsibility.

But other signs are disturbing. After a decade-long decline in casual drug use, we face a new and rising trend. Worse, the new wave of drug use is appearing in a younger group of children (fifteen or under). And the kind of young criminal the juvenile justice system must deal with today is much more chilling—not a young man who has messed up and regrets it, but a cold and hardened sociopath who some criminologists accurately describe as a "superpredator." Chuck Colson, who leads Prison Fellowship Ministries and who has walked into some of the darkest prisons in the world armed with only a Bible, freely admits that these new young criminals give him pause and almost destroy his hope. (*Almost* is the key word here. Chuck never gives up on anyone, which is why Prison Fellowship Ministries is one of the great engines of prison reform and criminal rehabilitation in the world today.)

Fortunately for us, we have only begun to utilize our most effective weapons in the national effort to heal people and thus drive down crime, illegitimacy, poverty, and hopelessness: the church and faith.

Most of our pathologies are rooted in fractured families that cannot pass along to their children the core values that allow for happy and productive lives. But if the values governing decent behavior are not being taught in our homes, our children need to learn them elsewhere. Many people are making a difference in their communities every day by providing moral and spiritual leadership to fatherless youths. For example, the Reverend Lee

Earl opened a church in one of the roughest neighborhoods in Detroit. Within ten years, he transformed the community from one centered on drugs, prostitution, and welfare into one centered on helping each other and trusting God. Small business and home ownership returned, crime rates fell drastically, and a community was reborn.

Most programs that succeed at steering children away from crime and toward productive lives are privately funded by religious organizations, institutions, or foundations. According to noted criminologist John J. DiIulio, "When you look at the gutbucket stuff, the everyday, in-your-face working with troubled kids in these neighborhoods across the country, almost all of it is being done by people who are churched."

Studies have consistently shown that children who have religious influences in their lives are much less likely to engage in substance abuse. For example, a four-year study conducted in the Rocky Mountain region demonstrated that religious involvement resulted in significantly lower rates of drug use, delinquency, and sexual promiscuity. Another study showed that church commitment was inversely correlated with violence. Likewise, neighborhoods with a high degree of religious practice are not high-crime areas, and youths in those neighborhoods are more likely to find jobs.

What's needed from the nation's leaders is a thorough commitment to allowing faith-based organizations to flourish. These cultural paramedics have the energy and the talent. They have the troops. But they need money and materials, and the federal government ought to push it to them by freeing state and local governments from any federal rules against aiding the most effective organizations in their midsts.

I have been a supporter of U.S.A. Harvest, a magnificent effort launched by stockbroker Stan Curtis in Louisville, Kentucky, to collect and share the vast amount of extra food this country produces every day. Most years U.S.A. Harvest collects more than 100 million pounds of "leftovers" and delivers them to the needy.

U.S.A. Harvest is not itself a "faith-based" program, but it welcomes alliances with people of faith. One client of the Memphis Harvest program told me of a pastor who volunteered there. Because of the pastor's involvement, that client who came to get *physically* fed found *spiritual* nourishment as well, and it was the latter that turned his life around. That's the impact of faith-based movements and those groups like U.S.A. Harvest that partner with them.

Opponents of aid to these faith-based programs are usually cheerleaders for big government and the bureaucrats who staff it. We tried that approach. We built huge buildings with thousands of desks and billions of dollars' worth of resources. And it didn't work. The Great Society was great in its budgets and great in its failures. Now it's time to put our money and our support where it will achieve actual gains.

That religious institutions and organizations are far outperforming the government in dealing with America's inner cities is a truth conceded by some of the most unapologetically liberal members of Congress. For example, Sen. Paul Wellstone of Minnesota admits that faith-based agencies have done some of the best work he has seen in this area. This is why he and several other Democrats in Congress joined the Republican majority in overwhelmingly voting in favor of the "charitable choice" provision in the welfare-reform bill. This provision allows local communities the option of replacing public welfare services with equivalent programs run by faith-based agencies. Providing poor and fatherless children not only with food, shelter, and education but also with moral leadership and example greatly increases the likelihood that those children will be law-abiding and productive members of our society.

In 1998, Reggie White arranged for me to visit a church-based gang-intervention program in Milwaukee. Reggie is a future Hall of Famer whose heart is as big as his body. Nothing scares Reggie, not even the daunting task of breaking through to hard-core gang members.

I sat around a table with about a dozen former gang members. A year earlier, they explained, they'd been shooting at one another with the very kind of weapons our urban areas have grown so wearily accustomed to. But now they were partners in job-training sponsored through Reggie's group and monitored by the church where we were meeting. Instead of shooting at each other, they were praying with each other.

That's real progress, produced by a real program. No government program can equal it.

7

Protecting Children

M Y YOUTH was spent in Phoenix, Arizona, and Huntington, a rural town in Indiana. Both were closely knit communities where many of the mothers stayed home and the children roamed around only under numerous pairs of watchful eyes. My schools were orderly and free of drugs and violence. Summer vacation meant loading a station wagon and driving off to a camp at a lake or park.

The dramatically different life led by today's youth is the result of an extraordinary shift in our culture's attitude toward children and young adults. A generation ago, it was taken for granted that society would act to protect the innocence of its members under the age of eighteen. Both the public and private sectors acted to keep young people sheltered from reckless and immature sexuality and safeguarded from making choices they were not mature enough to make wisely.

Nowadays, as Michael and Diane Medved point out in their book, *Saving Childhood,* "even the most conscientious and protective parents feel helpless when it comes to shielding the innocence of their children." Whether in inner city neighborhoods or wealthy suburbs, write the Medveds,

> families face the same fears. We worry not only about what might happen to our kids on the way to school but about what values they will learn once they get there. We're concerned not only with the threat of physical assault but with the emotional and moral battering our children endure from peers and the media. In short, we feel powerless to counteract the implacable social forces that push our own flesh and blood to grow up too soon—and too cynical. We may shower youngsters with every sort of material blessing and glitzy diversion, but we can't seem to give them the greatest gift of all—a secure, optimistic, and reasonably sheltered childhood.

It has become a herculean task to drain the swamp that has become youth culture. But we must speak out. As vice president, I strongly criticized Time Warner for peddling violent songs like "Cop Killer." Bill Bennett and his allies took the next step and confronted Time Warner executives with the lyrics of the rap music they were producing and distributing. Those executives should have stared at their shoes in shame.

We must try at least to offer our help to those parents who are struggling against this tide of rampant sex, violence, and pseudo-worldliness. Ironically, the campaign against youth smoking uses the same rhetoric as the defenders of youthful innocence. Sadly, I do not expect that the generals in the war against teen smoking will be taking a lead role in the effort to teach abstinence.

There nevertheless are certain crucial steps that must be taken to help protect the country's children from threats far worse than cigarettes.

RESPECT PARENTS' VALUES

Parents have the right to raise their children without interference from any level of government. Only if they abuse their children should the government step in. But where they are striving to bring up children with values in opposition to the culture around them, they must be allowed to do so without harassment.

Earlier I mentioned my sister-in-law's service on the Tennessee Textbook Commission. Bad as I already suspected things were, I was amazed to see the material she sent me about the scores of textbooks being used in school districts around the country. Book after book offers incredibly biased and distorted views on subjects ranging from natural history to environmental policy to American history and, of course, human sexuality. Those with a student at home should take the time to leaf through their child's textbooks. They are almost certain to be as dismayed as I was. Students are told, for example, that we "abuse land because we regard it as a commodity belonging to us"; that the world is horribly overpopulated and growth must be curbed "before the choice is between mass starvation and coercive measures that severely restrict human freedom"; that the nations of the world should submit to an "International Environmental Court" to settle environmental disputes; that many people are uncomfortable discussing sexual behavior because of the "puritanical roots of mainstream American society"; and that Presidents Ronald Reagan and Warren Harding are comparable because both were popular and led administrations "full of scandal and mismanagement."

Education should have nothing to do with ideology. Period. And parents have an absolute right to insist on non-ideological education for their children.

DRUGS

American families deserve real leadership in the fight against illegal drugs, and for the last six years that leadership has been lacking. The first indication of Bill Clinton's priorities came when he cut the drug czar's office by 80 percent, leaving it with less than half as many employees as the White House communications staff. The second indication was his appointment of Joycelyn Elders as surgeon general. Her repeated suggestions that the nation consider legalizing drugs went unrebuked by the White House.

Worst of all was Clinton's abandonment of the bully pulpit of the presidency. To this day, his most memorable pronouncement on the drug issue came during an appearance on MTV, where he laughingly replied, "Yes—I tried it before" when a high school student asked whether, if he could do it over again, he would "inhale."

In light of these failures, it was not surprising to learn that teenage drug use *doubled* during the first term of Clinton and Gore. Congressman Charles Rangel of New York, an outspoken Democrat, said that in nearly three decades in Congress, he had "never seen a president care less about drugs."

Renewed leadership in the fight against drugs must begin with a clear and simple moral message. We must, as James Q. Wilson has written, "speak plainly—drug use is wrong because it is immoral and it is immoral because it enslaves the mind and destroys the soul." And we must follow up with an appeal to personal courage for those times when temptation is strong. "Just say no," Nancy Reagan urged in the 1980s, and millions of American children did just that.

Strengthening the family, with its inherent support base, as well as improving moral education and treatment programs, will help us turn the corner in the drug war. But government alone has the job of providing the law enforcement and interdiction strategy necessary to keep drugs off our streets.

Some say the goal of a drug-free America is unrealistic. I admit that it won't happen overnight, but it's worth fighting for and that's what I'll do.

INDECENCY ON THE WEB

Anyone with a computer knows about the pervasiveness of pornography on the web. Pornography is even accessible on many local library terminals. We do *not* have to tolerate this. The 1998 Child Online Protection Act was a start, but we need to see it implemented and then go beyond it. Earlier this year a lower court put the act on hold, ruling that it violates the First Amendment. If an appeal fails, we will need new and better laws to punish pornography merchants who endanger the morals and mental health of children. And if the courts strike down these laws, we will need to try again and again. We mustn't fear the condemnation of so-called "sophisticated" opinion. I am concerned—and millions of parents along with me— about our children, and the pornography industry should be on notice that the days of easy distribution and easier profits are over.

HELPING PARENTS HELP THEIR CHILDREN

I've briefly touched on just three of the many concerns that parents have for their children. The pace of change in our technology-driven society will continually raise up new and unanticipated threats to our young people. We must, in turn, continually reevaluate the needs of our most vulnerable citizens, and we must always seek first the advice of parents on how to combat those threats and meet those needs. The most brilliant Ph.D. will never match the sincere concern of a loving parent, and it is the God-given responsibility of that parent to mold the life of his or her child.

8

Civil Rights in the Twenty-first Century

VERNON JORDAN and I share an alma mater in DePauw University, but I have not shared the struggle that he has lived. When Vernon told me years ago that as an undergraduate he had to drive forty miles to Indianapolis to get a haircut, I understood what Americans of all colors need to comprehend: The deep scars that racism has left upon our land will require generations of effort to eradicate fully.

It's a lesson I was reminded of again when my son and a good friend of his, who is black, were pulled over by police for an infraction my son could only describe as "driving while black." We are not yet a society that is color-blind. All Americans must recognize that not only was racism real, it is *still* real, and it must be fought and eliminated.

But only with the right weapons.

Civil rights laws should unite Americans, not divide them. They should guarantee equal opportunity but not mandate equal results. And they should be fair to everyone. Unfortunately, these common-sense propositions are often ignored today.

A Color-Blind Nation

I was pleased that the voters of California, responding to the leadership of Ward Connerly and others, passed the anti-quota Proposition 209 in 1996. The voters of Washington wisely followed suit two years later with Initiative 200. Both of these ballot initiatives bar the state government from practicing discrimination, including the use of any preferences based on race, ethnicity, or sex in contracting, employment, and university admissions. Courts in Virginia and Massachusetts have also recently recognized that elementary and secondary school districts cannot be allowed to prefer students or teachers of certain races to meet pre-ordained quotas.

There is a lot of confusion—deliberate confusion, I might add—regarding this issue. The people who resort to preferences frequently accuse those opposing them of wanting to "turn back the clock" on civil rights enforcement and of intending to eliminate all affirmative action. Neither charge is true, and both of them undermine the possibility of an honest, good-faith discussion of these important issues.

The laws passed in the 1960s prohibiting discrimination against anyone because of his or her skin color, religion, national origin, and sex are vital laws, and they must remain in place. They make it illegal to discriminate in a wide variety of settings, including employment, public accommodations, education, voting, and housing. Most of those opposing quotas and preferences vigorously support these laws and their effective enforcement. Certainly I do.

I also support taking aggressive steps to root out existing discrimination. We should encourage nondiscriminatory outreach and recruitment measures in a variety of settings such as private hiring, government contracting, and college admissions.

However, purposeful government discrimination is objectionable, and it is inconsistent with the ideals of the civil rights movement. Classifying individuals by race, ethnicity, or gender and then treating some of them better and others worse because of that classification is morally repugnant. This is plain discrimination, and it is wrong.

Such discrimination, unfortunately, is common. Both the public and private sectors use preferences in employment. Our federal, state, and local governments also frequently discriminate on the basis of race, ethnicity, or gender when they award contracts. And both our public and private colleges and universities make their admission decisions based in part on their applicants' skin colors and ethnic backgrounds.

Perhaps the most fundamental abuse of racial and ethnic classifications has been in connection with voting rights. Civil rights groups and the Department of Justice have distorted the Voting Rights Act, using it to require racial proportionality enforced by means of racial gerrymandering. This has led to the drawing of some voting districts so as to cram as many blacks as possible into them without considering whether they share a community of interest other than their race.

The inevitable result of practices like racial gerrymandering is to discourage interracial coalition building. Some Republicans, I am ashamed to say, have supported this perversion of the law because it sometimes works to their short-term electoral advantage. They are wrong to do so because in the long run it threatens to Balkanize our country.

To continue dividing Americans along racial and ethnic lines is profoundly unjust and unwise. And in a country as diverse and dynamic as America, it is ultimately impractical. Tiger Woods calls himself a Cablinasian, meaning Caucasian, black, Indian, and Asian. Ward Connerly is of black, Native American, and other ancestry. These two men represent a rapidly growing segment of America: those who cannot be accurately classified as belonging to any particular racial or ethnic group. In such a society, a governmental system of racial preferences would require definitions that are unworkable and unworthy of America.

In our great country, ethnicity and race should be sources of pride and tradition, not entitlement and resentment. The plain language of the Civil Rights Act of 1964 and the ideal that it enshrined bars discrimination against anyone—black or white, male or female, Hispanic, Asian, or Native American. Yet bureaucrats and federal judges have rewritten the law so that we now have a statute that prohibits discrimination against some groups (minorities, women) in just about any situation but allows discrimination in many instances against others (non-minorities, men). This clearly denies "equal protection of the laws" to some Americans, which the Fourteenth Amendment to the U.S. Constitution guarantees. The Supreme Court has ruled that such classifications are "presumptively unconstitutional." I would object to them as morally wrong even if they weren't also prohibited in most instances by the Constitution.

Yet the Clinton-Gore administration will not abandon its devotion to preferences and racial stereotypes. The next leader of the executive branch should insist that its agencies end this two-faced interpretation of the law and adhere to the Supreme Court's holding that rejected it.

The federal government should also pass legislation banning the use of racial preferences by any state or local government. This would do no more than fulfill the original meaning of the civil rights laws passed in 1964 and 1965—a meaning that was twisted and distorted by federal courts and bureaucrats and that continues to be resisted by many government officials today.

More than that will be necessary, however. Courts and government bureaucrats have also eagerly encouraged discrimination against some groups by interpreting the law to force employers to prefer certain other groups. According to these decisions, if an employer had a nondiscriminatory requirement for holding a job—say, holding a high school diploma—he could still be held liable for discrimination if that requirement had a disproportionate effect on a particular group. Faced with this legal atmosphere, employers feel they have to choose between expensive litigation to prove that the challenged practice is a "business necessity"—or else merely "hire by the numbers" to avoid being sued in the first place.

An important part of ending the use of preferences based on race, ethnicity, and sex is, therefore, to restore an ordinary definition of "discrimination." Employers and others provide equal opportunity, but they cannot be forced to guarantee equal results. To this end, I would propose that Congress provide an affirmative defense for employers who are able to document that they provide equal opportunity regardless of whether a particular proportion of some group exists in their work force.

The idea embodied in the Declaration of Independence that we are all created equal is based on the biblical notion that we are all children of God, equally beloved in His eyes. Certainly this country has not always lived up to this ideal, and for that transgression we have paid a terrible price, first in the evils of slavery, then in the slaughter of the Civil War, and then in the shame of Jim Crow. Martin Luther King Jr. dreamed of a land where people are judged not by the color of their skin but by the content of their character. So let us do everything we can to live that dream. Those who say we need to take account of race to get over race are simply consigning America to a never-ending cycle of resentment. We must focus on what we have in common, on what lies within us, not what is on the surface. In the words of boxer George Foreman, "I'm not black or white. I'm American."

We are all Americans.

9

Immigration

Any discussion of the values that made this country great must include a tribute to the openness with which America has received the world's émigrés and especially its refugees from want and war.

The words on the Statue of Liberty are not a cliché—they are the essence of America: "Give me your tired, your poor, Your huddled masses yearning to breathe free. . . . I lift my lamp beside the golden door!" America's experience with immigration has been miraculous. No other nation has so successfully combined peoples from every corner of the earth into a single, unified people. I am pro-immigration because, like almost every American, my ancestors came here from somewhere else. An immigrant sworn in today as a citizen is no less an American than the rest of us. As Ronald Reagan never tired of reminding people, no matter where you came from, once you are here, you can be an American.

America has been and, I hope, always will be a magnet for those who dream of better lives. And it has been a blessed refuge for those persecuted for their religious beliefs, their ethnic heritage, or their political affiliations. The immigrant spirit, exemplified by the courage required to leave familiar territory and seek out a new life in a new country, has added a rich texture to the American character.

Immigrants tend to be among the most hardworking and patriotic members of our society even as they contribute mightily to our growth and prosperity. Some of the most patriotic Americans I've encountered are refugees from Fidel Castro's regime. The Cuban-American community in southern Florida operates more than six hundred thousand businesses and generates ten times more income than Cuba itself. What a tremendous asset to our country.

Columnist Charles Krauthammer observes that immigration "illuminates one of the great paradoxes in American life: How is it that our schools are consistently among the worst in the developed world and yet we lead the world in science and technology and R&D in just about every field? The answer is simple. We import many of our best brains. Walk down any corridor in the laboratories of the National Institutes of Health, for example, and you'll meet the best young minds from every corner of the globe." A study by the Manhattan Institute found that today's immigrants are more likely to have intact families, earn college degrees, and be employed (and are no more likely to commit crimes) than are natural-born Americans.

In 1994, however, the issue of immigration exploded into American politics with a force not seen since the anti-immigration furor directed at Eastern Europeans in the 1920s.

In California, especially, an effort to take steps to halt what was perceived as a flood of illegal immigration (according to the Immigration and Naturalization Service, about 275,000 per year) led to the passage of Proposition 187, a lengthy laundry list of proposals to cut off government-provided benefits to illegal immigrants.

Proposition 187 was the result of public frustration at the federal government's indifference to the local costs of illegal immigration, and it passed overwhelmingly. The problem was that Prop. 187 struck many—even those sympathetic to the cause of controlling our borders—as having gone too far. It was a political disaster, and it cast a cloud over America's reputation as an open and generous country.

Proposition 187 is still tied up in the courts and may remain there for years to come. It's time to move beyond the events of the past and look to the principles that should guide immigration policy in the future.

Even the most eloquent advocates of immigration do not expect America to surrender control of its borders. Every country must exercise such control, and we have the technology to do it well. All elected officials must make clear that as a sovereign country, only the United States can decide who will and who will not enter our territory, on what basis, and for how long.

Furthermore, we must institute more strict workplace enforcement of the immigration laws. This doesn't mean that we have to embrace every big-government proposal (especially not national identification cards) that comes along. It does mean that we need to get serious about enforcing the laws we do have and about providing the resources necessary to do it. Half of all new illegal aliens in the United States each year actually entered the country with permission to live here temporarily but decided to continue working here in jobs they'd found. It is a matter of simple fairness—both to American citizens and to foreign nationals who are here legally—to take steps to end this practice. As Robert Hill, a member of the bipartisan commission on immigration policy chaired by the late Barbara Jordan, has said, "Serious enforcement at the worksite will reduce the pressure for more troublesome Prop. 187–like enforcement in neighborhood hospitals and schools."

I also believe that immigration policy should be more friendly toward the immediate family. Current law allows so-called "chain migration," under which a single immigrant can, through a chain of sponsorship, bring in a long line of far-distant relatives for entry into the United States. Aside from creating the impression that immigration is an entitlement rather than a privilege, chain migration results in huge backlogs that delay the unification of nuclear families, which should be our priority.

As our country remains true to its pro-immigration legacy, we must recommit ourselves to the overall vision of immigration: namely, Americanization—meaning simply that we must do everything we can to help new citizens assimilate into our common culture. As the Jordan Commission declared, "'Americanization' earned a bad reputation when it was stolen by racists and xenophobes in the 1920s. But it is our word, and now we are taking it back."

The need is especially acute in this age of "multiculturalism," in which elite groups lobby for ethnic separatism. We are headed for what federal appellate judge J. Harvie Wilkinson III calls "self-selected segregation." That is a terrible destination, and we must change course. We must assert once again, with confidence and a generous spirit, that America is a great melting pot. And we must strive harder to make the melting pot work. Schools, public institutions, and the culture at large should do a better job of reinforcing the meaning of citizenship and the importance of national unity.

At times the citizenship process has fallen victim to the modern tendency to emphasize rights over responsibilities and entitlements over duties. In her book *Americans No More,* Georgie Anne Geyer notes that when the INS put together a new version of the citizenship test in 1986, one of the questions asked the applicant to "Name one benefit of being a citizen of the United States."

There were only three acceptable answers: (1) to get a government job, (2) to obtain a passport, and (3) to have your relatives come and live here. No credit was given for answering freedom of speech, freedom of religion, freedom of association, or the opportunity to vote.

In a way, question 86 symbolizes what has happened to the concept of citizenship in America. We talk about the most material kinds of benefits rather than the great principles of our country. We focus on "what's in it for me" rather than the simple honor of being an American or the duties of citizenship.

It's worth reminding ourselves that citizenship is not just a bundle of rights. It is also a collection of responsibilities and duties: following the law, respecting fellow citizens, working hard, finding ways to serve your nation or community when you are needed, and taking responsibility for children you bring into the world.

These are values that all of us should be able to understand and live by. We are one country, bound together with a common destiny. A citizen can cherish his or her ethnic heritage but still be every inch an American—living, working, voting, and sharing in the incredible blessings afforded to the citizens of the greatest nation on earth.

That's what America means to the world. And as long as that remains true, I believe there will always be room for those who wish to join us.

10

Restoring Justice

I N THE BATTLE to restore middle-class values, I have left the most difficult task for last. We can win debates, we can achieve legislative victories, and we can succeed in citizen initiatives — but if a court decree nullifies our hard work, these victories will have been hollow indeed.

The next president will likely appoint at least three Supreme Court justices and several hundred lower-court federal judges. Choosing poorly could lead to a country in which the Supreme Court "discovers" a constitutional prohibition against school choice, or constitutional rights to partial-birth abortion and same-sex marriages, or more court-imposed rights for criminals. At stake also is the constitutionality of racial preferences and racial gerrymandering, as well as the question of whether there are any limits on Congress's power to invade state prerogatives. All that and more will turn on the next presidential election.

We face much more than isolated instances of judicial activism. By the time Bill Clinton leaves office, he will have appointed almost 60 percent of the federal judiciary and at least two Supreme Court justices. Many of these judges will seize the opportunity to legislate *their* liberal agenda. They will seek to impose *their* values on the rest of America. Legislating from the bench has been going on for years, and it must stop. Our Constitution gives the people, through their elected representatives, the right to pass laws. Judges may strike down the will of the people only where a provision of the Constitution has clearly been violated. Inevitably there are going to be cases where this question presents a close call, but the modern judiciary has crossed way over that line. Many judges feel empowered to act according to what Justice Oliver Wendell Holmes termed the "felt necessities of the times"—"necessities" that, not surprisingly, coincide with the policy views of the elite.

Here are examples of what is at stake.

Last year, the Senate failed by a narrow margin to override President Clinton's veto of a bill prohibiting partial-birth abortion. But even if Congress had overridden the veto, the Senate's efforts might have been rendered irrelevant by an arrogant Court striking down the law as unconstitutional. As I write this book, half of the states have adopted restrictions or outright bans on partial-birth abortion. In seventeen of those states judges have already blocked the enforcement of those laws. In many cases, the injunction is temporary pending the outcome of litigation. In some states, however, the injunction is permanent. The U.S. Court of Appeals for the Sixth Circuit, for example, has invalidated Ohio's ban on partial-birth abortion. The issue will soon be in the hands of the Supreme Court.

Parental choice in education is another critical issue that lies in the hands of judges. At least thirty-two states have adopted a school-choice program of some kind, and many of these programs are bogged down in court. Wisconsin is a good example. The school-choice program there began in 1990 and has proved a great success. Opponents of the program, however, have repeatedly asked courts to declare it unconstitutional—and some judges have. The ACLU, People for the American Way, and the NAACP joined the educational establishment in challenging a 1995 expansion of a program designed to offer choice to more parents. Although some lower court judges agreed with the ACLU and NAACP and declared the law unconstitutional, the Wisconsin Supreme Court recently reversed them. For now, then, there is school choice in Wisconsin, and the Supreme Court of the United States recently declined to review the state court's decision. Without an affirmative ruling from the highest court, however, that program and others like it remain vulnerable to the whims of lower court judges.

The sanctity of marriage has also become subject to judicial intervention. Judges in Hawaii and Alaska have announced a "right" to same-sex marriage. Voters objected so strongly to these rulings that both states recently passed referenda reversing the judges' decisions. The people were able to do this because these decisions were based on state law. They would not have been able to overturn the decisions, however, if they had been based on federal constitutional law. Not surprisingly, advocates of same-sex marriage are already mounting federal law–based challenges. Therefore, it would take the votes of only five liberal justices of the Supreme Court to declare a constitutional right to same-sex marriage—a right that every state and locality would then be compelled to recognize. This is no mere theoretical possibility; the Supreme Court has already held, astonishingly, that the people of Colorado may not prevent homosexuals from obtaining preferential treatment under state or local law.

The Supreme Court has also struck down state laws limiting the terms of congressmen from those states, guaranteed the right to air obscene material on cable television, and cast aside all-male military colleges. In similar activist mode, the U.S. Court of Appeals for the Tenth Circuit ruled that a teacher could not silently read the Bible at his desk in order to set a good example for his students.

Some judicial actions have directly undermined public safety. A federal judge in Philadelphia, for instance, ordered the release of several thousand prisoners on grounds that they were living in over-crowded jails. Within two years, criminals released under the judge's order were rearrested and charged with more than a thousand assaults, nearly a thousand robberies, over two thousand drug offenses, ninety rapes, and seventy-nine murders, including that of a police officer.

It's bad enough that federal judges should place themselves in charge of prison systems; it's totally unacceptable that judges consider themselves empowered to put dangerous felons back on the streets.

There are other critical issues still to be affected by judicial appointments: crime-control legislation, religious-freedom laws, pornography restrictions — these and still more will sooner or later come before the courts. The stakes, though, transcend any of these individual issues. Judicial activism is so pervasive as to threaten our right to self-government. Too many judges have effectively adopted the new aristocracy's position that the American people cannot be trusted to govern themselves.

Judicial nominations must be a central issue in the next presidential election, and I intend to raise it often. As Justice John Marshall Harlan explained, "The Constitution is not a panacea for every blot upon the public welfare, nor should [a] Court, ordained as a judicial body, be thought of as a general haven for reform movements." But so long as we elect presidents who appoint activist judges, courts will continue to legislate.

I will look for judicial nominees who clearly understand the proper role of federal judges. As Justice Felix Frankfurter wrote: "[I]t is not the duty of judges to express their personal attitudes on issues, deep as their individual convictions may be. The opposite is the truth; it is their duty not to act merely on personal views." A good judge, he continued, thus requires "perceptive humility . . . in not declaring unconstitutional what in a judge's private judgment is deemed unwise and even dangerous."

Humility is especially important. A judge, after all, wields much power and surely faces temptation every time he or she puts on a robe, enters a court, and is addressed as "Your Honor." The temptation is a natural one—and almost always takes the form of an impulse to do good. With the stroke of a pen, the judge can feel that he or she has fixed an injustice, improved an unwise law, or eliminated a dangerous one.

Thus, a potential judge's appreciation of the limits on judicial power should be the main focus of a nomination. People who humbly understand that they may not read their personal preferences into the Constitution are the ones I'd be looking for. However, on the important constitutional issues of our time, it would be absurd—and an abdication of presidential responsibility—to ignore whether a judicial nominee shares the president's philosophy of judging. In selecting a Supreme Court justice, on an important topic such as *Roe v. Wade,* I would want to know that a potential nominee regarded that decision as an exercise of raw judicial power. A person who failed to grasp that fundamental principle would hardly be likely to share my view that judges should not legislate from the bench.

The selection and confirmation process should not focus merely on "rights" but must also examine a potential judge's understanding of federal powers. The Constitution endows the federal government with limited powers, and we need more judges and justices who will recognize and enforce those limits.

To put all this a little more bluntly: We need more justices like Antonin Scalia and Clarence Thomas—and no more ringers.

Some judges, unfortunately, appear at first to recognize their limited role but suddenly "grow" in office to the acclaim of the elite (a process Judge Laurence Silberman dubbed the "Greenhouse effect," after the name of a *New York Times* legal correspondent). A president should only appoint judges who are already mature in their beliefs.

Each nominee to a federal court should be a person whose career reflects adherence to a firmly held set of principles and beliefs. A president must nominate individuals who understand the limited constitutional role of the judiciary, whose convictions are clear, and who are not easily swayed by the latest trendy legal theories.

Finally, a president who selects such nominees must also be willing to fight for their confirmation. As we learned in the battles over Robert Bork and Clarence Thomas, a principled conservative nominee will face vociferous opposition from those who want the federal courts to continue as superlegislatures. For the sake of the Constitution—and the integrity of the courts—we must fight back.

PART 3

Freedom and the Middle-Class Family

[T]here are more instances of the abridgment of the freedom of the people by gradual and silent encroachments of those in power, than by violent and sudden usurpations.

—JAMES MADISON

11

Protecting Freedom

U NTIL RECENTLY, the defining characteristic of this country
was the unparalleled freedom of its citizens. Today, however,
many see prosperity as the nation's defining characteristic. It is certainly true that our material wealth has made us more comfortable
than any generation in history, and that is a credit to the ingenuity
and enterprise of our people.

But it is not true that prosperity is the source of America's greatness. It is the freedom of a virtuous citizenry that defines us, binds
us together, and allows for prosperity. If we approach questions of
government from the perspective of enhancing our freedom, we
will be protected from making many serious mistakes, and we will
leave the way open for even greater accomplishments.

We must resist the temptation to grow complacent about the
blessings we enjoy as a free people. If we've learned anything about

public institutions over the last thirty or forty years, it is that gov-ernment is incapable of limiting itself. Even without encourage-ment, it has a natural tendency to insert itself into every aspect of our lives, further narrowing our freedom and our ability to chart our own destinies. This incursion happens gradually, even impercep-tibly, but the cumulative effect is dramatic. All of us have a duty to be ever mindful of threats to our freedom and the need to resist them wherever they arise.

For example, although many Americans are unaware of it, pro-posals abound that would give the government information about every aspect of our lives. Frankly, our private lives are none of the government's business.

The debate about "encryption," or coding, is one instance. This technology allows computer and cell phone users to communicate privately with codes that can't be understood by others. An e-mail message without encryption is kind of like a postcard in the mail: The recipient may not be the only one who reads it.

High-tech firms are developing encryption codes that are pro-gressively more sophisticated. As a result, the federal government has sought access to all encryption keys, arguing that key recovery is crucial to tracking criminal activity. The government is nowhere near proving the case that this would be necessary for effective law enforcement. And the bar should be placed high before we allow this type of invasion of privacy.

Nor is this the only disturbing threat to our privacy. Wiretaps have almost doubled under the Clinton-Gore administration, reaching a record high of 2.7 million in 1997. Congress has author-ized the Department of Health and Human Services to prepare "unique healthcare identifiers" for all Americans so that a national database of patient medical records can be created. Employers across America are required by law to submit the name, address, and social security number of every new worker to a government

"Directory of New Hires"—again, an easy way to create a federal database tracking every worker in the country. Recently issued federal regulations call for the development of social security cards that "shall employ technologies that provide security features, such as magnetic stripes, holograms, and integrated circuits"—a clear move toward developing a national identification card.

Another set of recently proposed regulations would have required every bank in America to keep detailed records on each customer's "normal" financial transactions and to notify federal authorities if the computers noted a departure from the "normal" banking pattern. Under these regulations, year-end bonus checks and withdrawals for down payments on home or college tuition could send up red flags! Grass-roots opposition, led by activists like Phyllis Schlafly, has stopped these proposed rules for now, but the entire episode reveals the intrusive impulses of the federal bureaucracy.

These measures may spring from good intentions. But each one of them requires another deposit of personal information into a government database. In an age when nine hundred raw FBI files—supposedly sealed by law—magically appear on the desks of political appointees in the White House, it is our right to question whether government can be trusted with the ability to track our medical records, our e-mail messages, our employment histories, or our movements throughout the country.

Sixty years ago, the average American's interaction with the federal government was confined to voting in elections and buying postage stamps. Now it is constant and wide-ranging.

We can't open a small business without having to hire lawyers and accountants to guide us through the paperwork. Nor can we do a thousand things we used to take for granted without first obtaining a government license or permit.

And the choices closest to our hearts—how we raise our children and how much time we spend with them—are restricted by a tax burden that falls so heavily on families that both parents are often impelled to work outside the home to make ends meet. When these types of outcomes are forced on us, we are less free.

But freedom is more than an end in itself. It also happens to be true—and I don't believe this is an accident—that the freedom enjoyed by a virtuous citizenry invariably produces the most effective ways of dealing with society's challenges. Whether it is free-market capitalism or the free exercise of religion or free speech, our nation is strengthened when millions upon millions of individuals exercise free choice rather than allowing a few self-anointed experts to make decisions for them.

On critical challenges such as federal taxation, healthcare, and education, proponents of the big-government philosophy have nothing to offer the American people except the status quo. The better answer is a vision that provides more freedom, allows greater choice, encourages individual initiative, and gets government out of the way.

When we focus on the preservation and expansion of freedom, we inevitably encourage growth and prosperity for all. Whenever we lose that focus, the policies and practices that follow inevitably make us worse off. No matter how difficult the task, the president must continually keep freedom as America's north star.

12

The Case for Tax Cuts

T HE TAX CUTS that Ronald Reagan pushed through Congress
in 1981 set off a genuine economic boom that has lasted, with
only a minor nine-month interruption, to this day. I was proud to
help with the passage of those tax cuts in the Senate. In the nearly
two decades since, the nation has become much wealthier and a
vast new group of Americans have become investors in the stock
markets or recipients of stock options and have reaped real returns
from the rise in the values of their shares. For many Americans,
there has never been a time of greater material prosperity.

ALL WORK, NO TIME

But this prosperity masks a number of other troubling developments that have been years in the making. Beginning in 1990, taxes

have been increased again and again. The relative value of deductions and exemptions—for dependent children, for example—has plummeted over the years. And the rise in incomes has pushed middle-income earners into higher and higher tax brackets.

The number of hours worked by our families has risen along with incomes. While we have always been a hardworking country, we also have carved for ourselves some days of rest. The weekends were for the home and the workday tended to begin at eight and end at five.

No more. Ours is now a seven-day-a-week, twenty-four-hour-a-day economy. A Cornell University study of two-career couples found that between 1972 and 1994, these couples' total average working time increased by seven hours a week—in essence, adding another entire workday to an already heavy burden. The same study found that more than 40 percent of men and 30 percent of women are working more hours than they want to. Why aren't they cutting back hours and taking a little less home in the paycheck? To me the answer is obvious: These couples need that income. There's no cushion in the family budget, so there's no leisure in the schedule. We have taxed our families into a position where every working hour counts. That must change.

Most Americans love their jobs and love their families but hate the juggling act in which they are caught. At best the money they make is necessary to continue living a life of modest comfort. Often it's the margin that keeps them from going broke.

It costs an enormous amount to live a middle-class life in the United States. By middle-class life I mean a decent house or apartment, a car, food, clothing, and a solid education for the children. Indeed, it now costs about $180,000 to raise a child through high school. I also include an annual vacation and a few nights out for Mom and Dad. The total package is not extravagant by any means.

One measure more than any other illustrates this: the cost of college. As even state-run colleges push tuition, room, and board into the range of ten thousand dollars and more per year, middle-class parents in America panic at the prospect of bright young sons or daughters being admitted to the college of their choice, only to find that the resources aren't there to send them.

Beyond the costs and beyond the fears, there is another issue: simple exhaustion. My assistant's husband, Don Minter, is a Nazarene pastor. I asked him earlier this year how people in his church were doing. His response: "As a pastor I can tell you that most Americans I meet are exhausted." He's right. We have accelerated the tempo of everyday life to the point that millions are missing dinner and leaving before breakfast.

Why? The American family is overtaxed. Federal taxes have ballooned by more than 70 percent over the course of the Clinton-Gore administration. Middle-class Americans are now sending the government almost forty cents out of every dollar they earn. That's outrageous. To the middle class, the tax code, as Ronald Reagan said years ago, is a daily mugging.

A dramatic tax cut would immediately strengthen the American family. It is long overdue. It is difficult enough to raise children, instill the right values, ensure a good education, and screen the TV and the Internet, without being forced to be absent too.

GROWTH AND OPPORTUNITY

I have always been an unapologetic member of my party's "growth" wing. I believe, as others have put it, that prosperity is a rising tide that lifts all boats. Such prosperity should always be our goal. Even now, at a time when the economy seems prosperous, not everyone is benefiting. Clearly, when more than 30 percent of young black men looking for a job are unemployed—as was reported in early 1999—there is much left to be done.

We need to raise our sights and aim higher. There is no reason why we cannot dramatically increase economic growth. And we should. A prosperous America where no one is left behind is an America better able to come to grips with pressures on the American family, with juvenile crime, and with the challenge of educating future generations of Americans. Dramatically increasing economic growth increases our ability to keep the promise of social security and expand individual freedom at the same time.

Reducing the tax burden on the middle class will help ensure that everyone who aspires to succeed in life has a real chance to do so.

Inevitably, liberals will denounce tax cuts as "giveaways" to the rich. Such grandstanding angers me for two reasons. First, the people who make this charge are typically well off themselves. They simply cannot imagine how a few hundred dollars more over the course of a year could greatly lighten a family's load—how it could spare a few tough choices or add a few nights out or a few days of vacation. Our upper-class elites have simply lost all connection with real working people. They worry about soccer moms to the exclusion of waitress moms. They shop at Nordstrom, but they somehow just don't see the salesperson at the counter or the truckdrivers delivering the goods.

Second, the charge that tax cuts unfairly benefit the wealthy is intellectually bankrupt. More good comes to everyone when money is invested in the private economy than when it is taken by the government through excessive taxation. When we reduce the tax burden we encourage investment and risk-taking on new ideas and new businesses. An entire industry—the high-tech revolution— was formed in the last twenty years because of this willingness to take risks, and our country is better for it, with literally hundreds of thousands of new jobs created.

Promoting American Freedom
through Tax Relief

Imagine a tax code that punishes success and rewards failure, that undermines the willingness to save, invest, or start a new business. Imagine a tax code that penalizes the decision by a man and woman to get married. Imagine a tax code that picks "winners" and "losers," not on the basis of what makes the economy grow or economic fairness, but according to the quality and reach of lobbyists.

Sadly, this describes the tax code that we have today. Far worse, however, is the fact that while both Democrats and Republicans largely agree that the tax code is defective, they have done nothing about it. In recent years, this has occurred because of the fiction—asserted by Clinton and Gore and swallowed by some gullible Republicans—that the current budget surplus must be used only to "save social security" rather than for tax cuts.

There is only one honest and effective way to protect social security: Take it completely off-budget. Stop the demagoguery. Stop raiding the trust fund and replacing the withdrawn money with paper IOUs. Put the social security money paid by workers and employers into a fund that will be untouchable for any other purpose. Washington politicians, who have over the years grown used to raiding the fund, keep resisting this fundamental reform.

Absent a serious recession, Washington is staring ahead at years of huge surpluses. Even as they pledge to use these surpluses to "save social security," Bill Clinton and Al Gore are lining up with special interests to siphon this money into new schemes to expand the federal government. It's the same old shell game. We need to couple the broad tax cut I propose with honest accounting in the social security trust fund.

Because of the complexity of the tax code and its bias against savings, and because of the drag on the economy from marginal tax rates that are too high, both the amount of taxes and the tax *code* itself keep America from achieving its full economic potential. We know that the moral and social fiber of our country is undermined by a tax burden that crushes lower- and middle-income families. We know, too, that the tax code discourages entrepreneurship.

But as important as these points are, the central issue is freedom and the size of government. Simply stated, big government fed by growing taxes reduces each American's control over his own life.

We must move to a flatter, fairer, and simpler system of taxation. That is why I propose the plan outlined below, which is sensible, easily grasped, and politically feasible. That it is also a dramatic plan will cause the usual suspects to scream that it is "risky," that the government "needs" the money. Let them scream. It's our money, not the government's. It is immoral for the federal government to confiscate from you a single dime more than is absolutely necessary. As the Democratic Party platform explained back in 1884, "Unnecessary taxation is unjust taxation."

A 30 Percent Tax Cut across the Board

I propose that we reduce marginal tax rates for individuals by establishing just three rates: in the case of joint returns, 10 percent for incomes below $44,000; 20 percent for incomes of $44,000 to $160,000; and 28 percent for incomes above $160,000. This would provide an average 30 percent cut in tax rates for every American, which I would phase in over a three-year period. Furthermore, I would simplify the tax code by eliminating all those unneeded tax preferences, credits, and deductions while preserving core deductions for interest on home mortgages, charitable contributions, healthcare, retirement, education expenses, and state and local taxes.

This plan would repeal the tax increases of the 1990s. A reduction in marginal tax rates would dramatically increase the incentives to save and invest, encourage productivity and entrepreneurship, and increase long-term growth. Equally important, it would keep middle-income earners from being pushed into higher tax brackets because of economic growth and higher personal earnings.

FREEDOM ACCOUNTS

I would also establish what I call Freedom Accounts, which can play an important role in easing the tax burden and thus in increasing the independence of the middle class.

Freedom Accounts would allow individuals to contribute up to ten thousand dollars annually in aftertax dollars with tax-free buildup for use in the retirement years. But Freedom Accounts as I visualize them are much more than supercharged IRAs. For I would also encourage the penalty-free use of these funds for four other important purposes: the education of a child at any school, whether it is a public, private, religious, or home school and whether at the elementary, secondary, or college level; the healthcare expenses for close family members; the costs of long-term care for elderly or disabled relatives; and the first-time purchase of a home.

In addition, all working Americans would have the choice of placing up to 30 percent of their social security payroll tax (or about 1.86 percentage points) into these Freedom Accounts. Such contributions would not count against the ten-thousand-dollar annual limit.

Freedom Accounts would create new incentives for savers to capture high investment returns, and they would provide new funds to finance technological and economic growth in the United States—and do so in ways that maximize individual choice and engage the genius of the free-market system.

And let's at long last improve and strengthen social security. There is a way for future social security beneficiaries to have more benefits without raising their already-high payroll taxes today. That way is to dramatically increase economic growth and personal choice. We cannot tax our way out of the long-term social security bind. The total payroll tax rate has already grown from just 2 percent in 1949 to 15.3 percent today. With social security "investment" returns currently in the range of 1 to 3 percent, it is imperative that we allow Americans the opportunity to invest some of their own money in the private sector with inflation-adjusted or real returns that can reasonably be expected to range from 5 to 7 percent. For ordinary Americans, this can make a huge difference in the quality of life they enjoy in their retirement years. For example, an American worker making $32,000 a year would—if he or she contributed only $600 a year—build a retirement nest egg of $155,000 after thirty-five years.

There are demagogues who will claim that this would undermine social security. The truth is quite the opposite. Those who opt for private investment under this plan would have an appropriate reduction in their social security benefits. Private investment, paid for by the surplus in current payroll taxes, can actually help ensure the long-term solvency of the system itself at the same time it allows Americans the freedom to increase their retirement savings. This is the first step toward putting social security on a sound footing for the twenty-first century.

REPEALING THE MARRIAGE PENALTY AND THE DEATH TAX

In addition to being simply unfair, both the marriage penalty and the death tax undermine some important values. The decision to get married ought to be made without reference to taxes, but there are more than twenty-one million married couples who get hit with an average penalty of fourteen hundred dollars a year because they chose to marry. During my first term in Congress more than twenty years ago, I recognized this problem and introduced legislation to correct this misguided tax policy. We must allow married couples the freedom to choose how they file—whether jointly or individually—whichever works to give them the most tax relief.

As for the estate tax, as my friend Congressman Chris Cox explains, it "seeks to repeal human nature." Nothing is more natural than that parents or grandparents, having built up a family-owned business or farm, should want to pass on the fruits of their lives' work to their children or grandchildren. But steep death-tax rates, ranging from 37 to 55 percent, often ensure that a lifetime of work simply evaporates in a check to the U.S. Treasury. This is a tax on hope for the future. It promotes consumption over saving and penalizes thrift. It must be repealed immediately.

Promoting Investment and Economic Opportunity

I also propose that we reduce the corporate and individual capital gains tax by 30 percent. I would also neutralize the current bias against investment by reducing the top corporate income tax rate to 28 percent and by allowing businesses to deduct taxes paid on dividends in order to minimize double taxation of corporate income.

The American people are smarter than the media would have us believe. Time and time again, the people of this country have shown they understand that punitive taxes on those who can invest in the economy only hurt those who want the opportunity to climb the economic ladder of success.

REFORMING THE IRS

In 1998, the Republican Congress, overcoming the initial objections of the Clinton-Gore administration, enacted a series of long-overdue reforms of the Internal Revenue Service. Those reforms represented a significant improvement, providing about seventy different ways to strengthen the rights of taxpayers, including the crucial shift of the burden of proof in court cases away from the taxpayer and onto the IRS.

I am, of course, committed to those reforms and several others besides. The IRS should publish a quarterly update of its efforts to comply with the new reforms. Congress should hold annual oversight hearings of the same sort that mobilized public opinion to press for reforms in the first place.

As president I would appoint a treasury secretary and IRS commissioner who represent the growth wing of the Republican Party and who are absolutely committed to keeping the IRS on the path of reform. The attitude at the top matters. My early work experience included a job as director of the inheritance tax division of the Indiana Department of Revenue. Lots of close calls arise in every tax agency at the local, state, and federal levels, and they certainly came up in my division. My standing orders to the staff were simple: Close calls and "ties" went to the taxpayer. My future appointees would carry this same preference for taxpayers into their jobs, and that attitude will make the additional reforms I implement even more effective in protecting hardworking Americans who pay their fair share in taxes.

When I left office in 1993, I expected that an IRS audit would follow. Given the relentless partisanship of the Clinton-Gore team, anything less would have startled me. The demand for an audit came almost instantly that same year. So Marilyn and I duly assembled the vast amount of material needed to respond to the government. It turned out that we had overpaid.

I *was* startled, however, when the agency came back with another demand for an audit the very next year. Again we assembled our proofs. This time the IRS decided that we owed an additional four hundred dollars or so—because of a deduction that the IRS believed should be taken in the next year—but only after the sort of ridiculous and wasteful paper chase that drives so many hard-working and honest Americans to distraction. I can assure you the government spent a lot more in time and effort than it got back with my four hundred dollars, which it had to turn around and give me a year later. If I had had the time, I would have fought paying even that amount, because the agency seemed driven to nail me for something only to save face, the kind of gesture that has become the trademark of the IRS.

Having suffered through seven audits, I know the excesses of the IRS. I am on the taxpayer's side.

Naturally, there are some tax cheaters out there, and they drive up the cost of government for all of us. But most Americans are honest and ready to comply with the revenue laws to the extent those laws can be understood.

It is very clear what we must do. The tax code is so cluttered with minutiae and special-interest loopholes that even accountants have trouble agreeing on what all the rules mean. As of last year, the tax code encompassed 5.4 million words, required 2,134 pages of law and 5,439 pages of regulations to explain, and necessitated the use of 480 different forms. I began fighting for tax reform close to twenty years ago. In 1982, I first proposed a major overhaul of the tax code that would have radically reduced its complexity. As president I will fight for such an overhaul.

13

Healthcare:
Freedom and Choice

M ANY AMERICANS believe things aren't quite right with the healthcare system. It's not so much an issue of quality; American healthcare is still the best in the world. Americans are concerned about whether they'll have uninterrupted coverage between jobs. They're worried that their decision to take a new job will be dictated more by the healthcare benefit package than the quality of the job, the location, or the salary. And millions are distressed when managed healthcare plans come between them and their doctors, fill their lives with confusing rules and restrictions, and make them follow procedures that are every bit as frustrating as dealing with the IRS.

The Medicare system, which should be a source of comfort for the elderly, is now a source of growing anxiety as the costs of the system spiral out of control. And baby boomers are discovering a new reality: the increasing need to provide for the long-term care of aging parents.

Healthcare is another of those issues where we seem to spend a lot of time wrangling and building plan upon plan, only to discover that we've made the problem worse. It is a rule of thumb with me that seemingly intractable problems can be solved by returning to first principles. In this case, as in so many others, the first principle is freedom. If we keep our eyes on that goal, encouraging patient choice, enhancing the freedom to contract with the providers and insurers that best meet the needs of families, and eliminating distortions in the federal tax code, I believe we will give the American people the healthcare they want and should have: healthcare that is affordable, portable, and accessible.

With the best healthcare system in the world, how is it that so many Americans have wound up with no healthcare insurance coverage at all or find themselves in plans they don't like? The fault lies with the federal income tax code. The code allows employers to fully deduct the cost of health insurance for employees, but this deduction is not yet fully available to individuals who buy their own insurance.

Those without healthcare coverage need help. We should ensure that everyone is able to exclude healthcare-coverage premiums from taxable income. Those who do have healthcare coverage need greater control over benefits, especially since higher healthcare costs have led more and more employers to select managed-care plans. And managed care often means jumping through endless bureaucratic hoops and spending hours on the telephone trying to get straight answers. Managed care also means that someone else determines the type and quality of care we are able to buy. For some, managed-care plans are the ideal choice. The point is that we need to ensure that every family has the opportunity to choose a coverage plan best suited to meet its needs. Given the option, many employees would take the money their employers now spend on a plan and find their own health insurance plans, or simply purchase their own healthcare directly.

Our goal, ultimately, should be individual ownership of all healthcare coverage, much as individuals own their own car insurance policies now. Individual ownership would provide greater choice and, by enhancing competition, help drive down healthcare costs.

I also support the concept of medical savings accounts, or MSAs, which allow greater patient control over healthcare expenditures. An individual could choose to purchase a less expensive, high-deductible health insurance plan and deposit the premium savings into a tax-free MSA. Those funds would be available for routine medical procedures throughout the year, and whatever wasn't spent would be available for medical expenses later. This reform would strengthen the patient's control over his or her care because each patient would deal directly with his doctor and make his own decisions about which treatments are worth paying for out of the MSA. The Freedom Accounts I've proposed in my tax plan will accommodate the best features of MSAs.

It is not surprising that many Americans are frustrated with managed-care plans. They want the freedom to move to insurers that respond to their concerns, respect their decisions, and don't intervene in their relationship with their doctor. The way to reach this goal is to encourage competition. What we must not do is embrace the many piecemeal attempts to enact the Clinton health plan of 1994, which would have put the federal government in charge of our coverage, our care, and our range of choices in physicians—creating, in effect, one gigantic, national managed-care organization.

Americans knew in 1994, and are certain today, that the big-government model of healthcare would be a national nightmare. Unfortunately, Bill Clinton and Al Gore have been implementing their scheme step by step; the president bragged in 1997 that he'd already achieved 60 percent of what he'd originally sought. We'll all be better off if we keep big government out of our doctors' offices.

AGING PARENTS

As the baby boomers grow older, they are being confronted with one of the most challenging transitions in life: the aging, illness, and death of beloved parents. This transition strains the physical, emotional, and financial resources of even the closest and most loving families.

I know too well the emotional and physical strains of a parent with serious long-term needs. A few years ago, my father, then seventy-six, fell as he was coming out of a convenience store. He struck his head, and his physical decline after that was rapid. He could no longer be cared for by my mother at home, so he is now in a long-term care facility.

We are blessed that my family can cope with the costs of my dad's care. It is hard for me to imagine how this difficult situation could be handled if his care had created a financial crisis.

The challenge of caring for America's elderly comes in three parts.

First, families need support as they struggle with this transition. The kind of support I am talking about is very much a matter of community and church, not government. But only if we as a society act to strengthen these institutions across the board can they be prepared to play their crucial role in the care of the elderly. Nothing, of course, can truly replace the family as a source of care and attention.

Second, we need to have an infrastructure of private facilities that deliver high-quality care.

Third, we need to help ensure that American families have the means to pay for long-term care or long-term care insurance. The most obvious step the federal government can take, of course, is to allow families to keep more of their own money so they can then place that money in savings for the purpose of paying for the long-term care of parents who need it.

When I began to draw up my tax plan, I realized that the Freedom Accounts so central to my plan must allow for the accumulation of tax-free savings that could be used, if the need arose, to contribute to the care of a parent or other close relative. I will not budge on this issue. This is a clear priority.

14

Education:
Restoring Accountability,
Standards, and Discipline

MARILYN AND I now ruefully refer to ourselves as "empty
nesters." Our two sons have graduated from college, and our
daughter will graduate next year. I am most thankful that we were
able to provide them with a good education.

The five families I interviewed in writing my previous book, *The
American Family: Discovering the Values That Make Us Strong*, were
very diverse, separated along racial, geographic, and socioeconomic
lines. But all agreed that, when it came to their children, education
was the top issue in their everyday lives. Education was what these
parents thought most about, talked most about, worried most
about, and prayed most about.

Parents really want several things from the K-through-12 education system. We want our children to be safe and disciplined while in school, and we want to be sure that they can get good jobs (or be equipped to go on to higher education) when they get out. We also want them to be motivated to learn, because we know both instinctively and from experience what Ralph Waldo Emerson meant when he said that education is "not the filling of a pail but the lighting of a fire." To paraphrase Margaret Thatcher, we want education to be part of the answer to our country's problems, not part of the cause.

America leads the world in per-pupil education spending, yet in a recent comparison with twenty-eight other advanced countries, American eighth-graders finished seventeenth in science and twenty-eighth in math. (The Czech Republic, in contrast, spends one-third the amount per student that we do, yet ranks second in science and sixth in math.) Six in ten Americans believe academic standards in their schools are too low. And 90 percent of American executives say that one of the most serious problems involving young employees is functional illiteracy.

In response to all of these problems, the education establishment—and by that I mean state and federal bureaucrats and teachers union bosses—keeps offering the same old solutions: more money, more administrators, more regulations, more surveys, more new programs. Their intentions are occasionally good, but too often they are simply self-serving. Their thinking never seems to go beyond granting more authority to the federal government and removing more freedoms from the states, communities, and parents.

You will not be surprised to learn that I take the opposite approach. Education is a national concern, but it is a state and local responsibility. Most important, education is the *parents'* right and duty. Common sense dictates that parents and institutions at the state and local levels—those closest to children—are better able to determine what is in the children's best interests.

When in Congress, I voted against the creation of a federal Department of Education because I believed that giving the federal government this kind of leverage would sooner or later translate into a power grab. And, as I write this book, President Clinton has shown just how he intends to accomplish the objectives of liberal elites. He'll do it by stealth—by telling states and local school districts that they cannot receive federal funding unless they implement certain preferred policies. Some of those policies may be good ideas. But if the federal government can force good policies on our local schools, it can impose bad policies on them too.

I believe the proper course is simple: Take most of the money spent by the federal government on elementary and secondary education and send it back to the states, insisting that at least 95 percent of that money be spent in the classroom in any way the states and local school districts see fit and not on administrative overhead that exists only to handle the complex regulatory requirements of the federal bureaucracy. If local schools want to hire more teachers, let them. If they want more computers or need a new building, they can choose that too. Or they can reduce class sizes. No matter how they choose, they will be answerable to the parents and accountable for the results.

Accountability is the basis of academic excellence. Standards are a good idea, but I oppose any mandatory national program of standards and testing; this is just another invitation to consolidate power in Washington. I do support the idea of states creating benchmarks to allow parents to compare student performance among schools, cities, and states. It is the role of parents, school boards, and educators to decide how best to deliver a quality education in their communities.

Accountability also requires that superintendents be allowed to respond to problems in their districts; they deserve the backing of the community when they do. Several years ago, the Indianapolis public schools superintendent warned that she planned to dismiss a number of principals at the end of the school year unless their schools showed improvement. Her position was simple: I was hired to make the system more accountable, and I take that job seriously. There was quite an outcry from the principals and the teachers union, but the school board supported the superintendent (though narrowly). A superintendent who demands accountability should be supported, not attacked.

Another necessary reform is teacher accountability. All the teachers I know work hard, and many of them are not paid enough. They should not be forced to carry their colleagues who aren't performing, nor should students be forced to suffer the consequences. It's ridiculous that in New York City it takes an average of 476 days (and an expenditure of $194,520) to remove a teacher for misconduct. I believe the revision of tenure laws is an unstoppable reform, and I intend to do everything I can to support that effort. Moreover, I would ensure that no federal law stands in the way of state efforts to establish teacher-testing and merit-pay programs, even with federal funds. Education reform should not focus exclusively on weeding out poor teachers—we need to reward the good ones too.

We all remember the teachers who had the biggest impact on our lives—the ones who helped us realize the satisfaction that comes from working hard, pushing ourselves, and seeing the fruits of our efforts. What struck me most about my favorite teacher was that she always seemed to be working every bit as hard as I was. My aunt, Sue Ott, was that way too. She was a public-school teacher in Indiana for more than forty years. I still marvel at how devoted she was to her job. She was at her school from early in the morning until late in the day. She loved children, and since she never married, her students were her family. Her dedication was total.

That's the life of the average teacher: sustained hard work. I realize that sometimes we ask too much of them. Nowadays, they find themselves filling out piles of needless paperwork, and they have been asked to take up the slack where the family is failing.

If we want teachers to teach and to be accountable, we need to give them the authority to maintain order in the classroom. We must give principals the authority to maintain order in the school building. I am unapologetic about supporting teachers' rights to impose effective discipline. Schools need behavioral standards every bit as much as they need academic standards.

We must also have the courage to recommit ourselves to teaching the basics of simple morality. An ethics professor in Phoenix recently told the story of a poll of young people between the ages of eighteen and thirty-four. Question: "Do you believe there are absolute standards of morals and ethics, or does everything depend on the situation?" Seventy-nine percent answered that there are no absolute standards.

Last year, a survey of twenty thousand students reported that 70 percent admitted cheating on a test and 47 percent said they had stolen something from a store.

To revive the moral sense in our young people, one thing we should strive for is an honor code in every school.

I don't mean one that's buried in a student handbook that everybody looks at once and then forgets. I mean an honor code that is posted and is part of each student's everyday life. Don't lie; don't cheat; don't steal, not even when it saves you embarrassment or seems like the easy way out. No federal involvement is needed here; no honor code mandates, no federal honor code agency, no honor code budget. It's not an issue of budgets or mandates but one of leadership. The president can use the bully pulpit of his office to stress that a quality education is more than just the "three Rs" of reading, writing, and arithmetic. The schools of America should reinforce two other Rs as well: respect and responsibility—and values such as honesty, integrity, and hard work. No lesson is more important.

15

Parents in Charge

I WILL FIGHT for a strong, vibrant public school system. Marilyn and I are both products of public education. For generations of Americans, a free public education was the first real break they got in life. Most parents want their children to attend the neighborhood public school and don't consider other options.

My goal is to make it easier for parents to do what they feel is best for their children's education. One way of doing this is through Freedom Accounts, which I outlined earlier. Though Freedom Accounts are first and foremost a tool for a secure retirement, they would also permit the withdrawal of funds for education expenses.

I purposely avoid specifying what expenses can be eligible for education in a Freedom Account, because there are a thousand different needs implied by the word *education,* and parents will know those needs better than anyone. If a parent thinks a home computer will help, he or she can buy it with funds in a Freedom Account. If a child has costs associated with after-school care or a special need for some tutoring, a parent can use the funds for those purposes too.

If the cost of a private education is at issue, Freedom Account funds could help there as well. This would apply equally to religious schools or to home schools. Freedom Accounts would enable millions of parents to strengthen their children's educational progress.

A congressional study last year showed that a similar type of account would, in most cases, be used by parents with students in public schools. And the vast majority of parents using these accounts would have incomes below seventy-five thousand dollars a year. In other words, the middle class would benefit the most from Freedom Accounts.

But we must remember that there are other parents in even more difficult circumstances who need extra help.

Picture a single mother living in the inner city with an eight-year-old daughter. Every morning, mother and daughter walk to the bus stop together. They hold hands until the moment the child climbs aboard the bus. At the school entrance, the little girl walks through a metal detector. She knows all the latest news involving drugs, gangs, and guns. In her school, as in many urban public schools, the majority of students who make it to the twelfth grade are functionally illiterate.

What an awful position for a mother to be in. And how much worse it must be for this mother when she knows there is literally no alternative available to her. She can't afford to move. She can't afford private-school tuition. She and her daughter are trapped.

Does it give this mother any comfort to hear a politician telling her that someday, if we spend enough money and try out enough different educational fads, schools like her daughter's will be better?

Can it conceivably make any difference to her that Al Gore promises to wire every classroom to the Internet?

Such promises can only add to her despair. That is precisely what I heard a few years back from an African-American woman in Chicago who told me she was tired of seeing children in her neighborhood having to attend schools that are nothing more than "factories of failure."

That's why I support school choice. I'm open to any good, common-sense idea for improving every public school in America. But I care even more about giving hope to children who are being utterly left behind by the system.

The Reverend Floyd Flake, pastor of the African Methodist Episcopal Church in Queens, New York, and a former congressman, has aptly described parental choice as the means of reaching "the final phase of civil rights," that is, economic power. "We cannot get to the economics without getting to the education."

He's right: This is a civil rights issue. It is also a struggle between the elites who presume to know more than parents do about what is best for the children of America and a growing cadre of concerned parents and citizens who have refused to take no for an answer. And despite all the media opposition and all the stonewalling by education experts and teachers unions, the grass-roots activists are finally beginning to win.

Leadership on school choice is provided both by grass-roots activists and by visionary public officials like Wisconsin's Gov. Tommy Thompson and Florida's Gov. Jeb Bush. Private-sector leaders have taken the initiative as well. In Ohio, businessman David Brennan found that one-third of his employees were illiterate and two-thirds were incapable of doing basic mathematics. Instead of losing hope, he developed a remedial education program. When public schools wouldn't give the program a try, he opened "Hope Academies" that are providing new educational opportunities for the disadvantaged. Theodore Forstmann and John Walton have created a nationwide scholarship program for low-income students. Even though the scholarships require a parental contribution averaging one thousand dollars per student—a huge sacrifice for poor families—the program had more than a *million* applicants this year for forty thousand openings.

For the most part, the school-choice movement has concentrated on the idea of vouchers: that is, taking federal or state education funding and offering lower-income families a voucher they can use for the specific purpose of paying for the costs of education at a private school.

At the federal level, the proper role of vouchers is a small one. Though I support wholeheartedly the idea of vouchers for low-income families, I do not want the federal government to administer such a program. I support what my good friend, former Sen. Dan Coats of Indiana, has proposed: making clear that the existing federal funding programs can be used, at the option of state and local communities, to support school-choice programs in those communities.

The real battleground for education reform is in the states, and this is where we've seen many profiles in courage, especially in cities like Milwaukee and Cleveland. Opponents charge that the choice movement is an attack on public schools. It is not. It may be the rejection of a specific school or school system that is failing its children, but the concept of public schools is a good one—one that the overwhelming majority of Americans support. Americans have the right to send their children to schools that work. And if they do not work, we should ensure that parents have the means to try something different.

In the meantime, we cannot allow another generation of children, particularly those in the inner cities, to be lost. I started visiting school-choice schools several years ago. It's hard to overstate the depth of feeling one finds in the parents of these students. It's a combination of hope, excitement, amazement, and above all, relief. Finally, the parents have control, and their sons and daughters have a chance!

A few years ago, in a debate televised by PBS, a Clinton White House aide, Bill Curry, made the following stunning declaration:

> Show me a system where all the parents are in the top percentile of income, and I'll show you a bunch of kids who, by and large, are on their way to Harvard. Show me a school system whose parents are in the bottom percentile of income, and I'll show you a bunch of kids on their way to jail.

Also in the room was Brother Bob Smith, the principal of Messmer High School, part of Milwaukee's school-choice program. He turned to Curry and said:

> I take offense at that, and the fifty graduates at my high school last Saturday take offense at that. Of those fifty graduates, 95 percent are African American and Hispanic, 70 percent low income, 70 percent single-parent family. They are not on their way to prison. They are on their way to college.

That's the school-choice debate in a nutshell: arrogant policy elites versus inner city parents, teachers, and principals who are actually getting the job done.

I am also encouraged by the success of charter schools in different parts of the country. Charter schools are semi-independent, publicly funded schools exempt from most state and federal bureaucratic regulations. In exchange, charter schools commit to meet explicit performance goals. Outside contractors—often parents, teachers, colleges, nonprofit groups, or museums—manage these schools under the oversight of a sponsor, such as a school board or agency. Charter schools have instilled a healthy spirit of competition. In Mesa, Arizona, for example, full-page newspaper ads have appeared, touting the virtues of the local public schools. In Lansing, Michigan, the public schools have won back several hundred students who had left the system to go into charter schools. That's what competition is all about. And who benefits? The students themselves and America as a whole.

Another recent development has been the increasing number of parents who home-school their children. Sometimes this choice is pressed upon a family because the lessons of the local public school system have become so antithetical to the values of the parents that they face a real dilemma: teach the children themselves or abandon them to the pressure of a culture that is hostile to their own values. Thousands of families have chosen home-schooling, and it is one of the most striking examples in modern times of a grass-roots response to cultural collapse.

It is also a visible rebuke to the education establishment, and the education elites have responded angrily. It's not an exaggeration to say that home-schooled children and their parents are discriminated against. Pundits and self-described education experts deride them. In state after state, though home-schoolers have succeeded on scholastic tests, they are met with burdensome regulations or phony qualification requirements that have only one real purpose: to discourage those who would have the temerity to take their children out of the public school system. What is significant is that despite these challenges, home-school parents have persevered and their children have prospered.

I can personally testify to the successes of home-schooling. My cousin Russ Pulliam and his wife, Ruth, home-school their six children, all bright, talented youngsters. It is clear that each of them is going to succeed in life. In every other home-school family I know, the children are respectful, responsible, well read, and more often than not, better prepared for college than any other single group of children in America.

It is a lesson worth emphasizing. There is more to teaching than opening a book. Love and personal attention are indispensable to a child's educational success.

Home-schooling may not be for everyone, but it ought to be a choice available to parents. I will defend every parent's right to that choice. As I have already noted, I would ensure that Freedom Accounts are also available for use by parents who home-school their children. And the first week I am in office, I will direct the new secretary of education to conduct a department-wide audit for obstacles to home-schooling. Then we will act to dismantle these obstacles. All the education "experts" in the country combined will never shake my confidence in parents.

Putting parents in control—through Freedom Accounts and school choice—is critical to the vision of restoring educational excellence. Of course, expanding these opportunities will not change the fact that public schools will continue to educate most of our children. We must dedicate ourselves to restoring them to their former excellence. But for children who are in trouble now, action is required immediately.

A few years ago, I read a book called *Our America*, written by two young men who had grown up in a housing project in Chicago. One of them wrote, "I live in a second America—an America that doesn't wave the red, white, and blue flag with fifty stars for fifty states. I live in a community that waves a white flag because we have almost given up."

No one in America should have to give up, especially not young people who are just beginning to make their way in the world. Greater educational choices for parents—and the means to make those choices—will help guarantee that our young people are full stakeholders in American society.

PART 4

America and the Global Economy

If we look to the answer as to why for so many years we have achieved so much, prospered as no other people on earth, it was because here in this land we unleashed the energy and individual genius of man to a greater extent than has ever been done before.

— RONALD REAGAN

16

Exporting Freedom

THE INTERNATIONAL economy depends upon the American economy, and the American economy depends upon the entrepreneurial energy and the spirit of innovation that increase productivity and enhance our quality of life. That energy and those innovations flow from the freedom that allows literally millions of dreamers, inventors, and builders to chart their own destinies and take their own risks.

The scale of economic change we are now witnessing surpasses even the massive shifts brought about by the industrial revolution. The entire world is now positioned to reap the benefits of the rise of new information technologies and the fall of imperial communism. We are on the verge of the greatest expansion of economic growth and prosperity the world has ever seen.

This will not be possible without American leadership—technological, political, and, yes, moral. America continues to be the hope of the world, and we can and should make good on that hope. I agree with those who look to a new century of American leadership on the global scene. We share the vision that the new millennium will unfold as an era of prosperity founded on American ideas and rooted in America's lasting democratic values—a century, as Jack Kemp has put it, that makes real the promise of a golden age of democracy, peace, and equality of opportunity, not only in our country, but throughout the world.

I welcome the challenge of American global leadership because I have absolute confidence in our ideals and institutions. The great lessons of America's national experience are not secrets that have to be closely guarded and concealed from others—far from it. We should export them. A world in which American ideals continue to spread and flourish will be a far better place for billions of human beings.

We know what works. Low tax rates, stable currencies, limited government, and the rule of law are the engines of prosperity. This is as true for other nations as it is for the United States. Yet our policies—and the international institutions our tax dollars support—sometimes run counter to these ideals. The result is that in a time of American prosperity the economic news is not so rosy in many other parts of the world. According to a recent report by the World Bank, growth in the developing nations' economies will average only 1.5 percent in 1999, well below their average population growth. We need to encourage faster growth in those countries, because the international economy, for good or ill, affects America's wealth and security.

We need leadership that will stand firm for the principles of freedom and democracy, promote the expansion of free trade, and have the courage to say no to outmoded international bureaucracies that thwart progress and worsen international economic problems.

EXPANDING MARKETS FOR AMERICA

Free trade is in America's best interest. The most prosperous times in our history (and other countries' as well) have been those when trade expanded: from 1873 to World War I; the 1920s and the 1960s; the Reagan boom from 1983 to 1990; and the early stages of the post-NAFTA period in the 1990s.

It's easy to understand why this is true. Free trade benefits consumers by reducing prices. It benefits producers by opening new market opportunities that translate into more jobs and greater prosperity for their communities.

Free trade rewards investment in innovative technologies and strengthens our most competitive industries. We've certainly experienced this firsthand in the United States with our substantial trade surplus in high-tech goods. Free trade continues to create and sustain tens of millions of high-paying American jobs.

We have every reason to seek to open more markets and promote growth around the world. Right now, our taxes on foreign imports are near zero. What we need is a strategy for cutting or eliminating foreign taxes on our exports and taking maximum advantage of the incredible opportunities now open to us in the areas of agriculture, services, and high technology.

Unfortunately, the Clinton-Gore administration has done very little to advance an agenda for opening up trade. The North American Free Trade Agreement (NAFTA) was negotiated before Clinton and Gore took office, and it passed only because of Republican support in Congress. Following ratification, the Democratic administration went back on a commitment to Chile to negotiate Chile's joining NAFTA. The administration further failed to get Congress to renew the "fast-track" negotiating authority needed for new agreements. The administration claims to have completed more than two hundred trade agreements, but at least a third of these are measures that actually restrict trade.

On trade issues, the Clinton-Gore administration is best known for two things: giving its political supporters preferential treatment on trade missions and loosening export controls under political pressure and without regard to the needs of national security.

It's time for leadership that takes seriously the opportunities before us and pushes a free-trade agenda that puts the national interest ahead of special interests.

There are those who contend that America should adopt a free-trade stance without regard to the trade practices of other governments. I agree with that view, up to a point. By the same token, however, I don't believe America should sit idly by when American manufacturers are victimized by trade partners engaging in clearly illegal practices. Last year, it became clear that the pampered steel industry in Japan and some developing nations was dumping steel on the U.S. market. It hit our steel industry fast and hard, resulting in layoffs of at least ten thousand workers. The administration's response was the typical "ready, aim, aim, aim, aim."

I am convinced that free trade is the best policy for America and the world. I also believe, however, that preserving and expanding America's global economic position is as fundamental a task as safeguarding the country from military attack. The remarkable openness of our economy helps keep our industries at the peak of competitiveness, but we would be foolish not to insist that the playing field be level. There is no need to revive the disastrous protectionist policies that helped create the Great Depression in the 1930s. But when America is the victim of flagrant trade violations, the president has a duty to fight those abuses with every tool at his command.

REFORMING INTERNATIONAL INSTITUTIONS

Exporting freedom also means promoting a combination of sound monetary, fiscal, and trade policies built around the objective of robust, noninflationary economic growth. We know from experience that such policies lift all boats at home and abroad.

As the one nation everybody else looks to for guidance in managing the world economy, America must insist on fundamental reforms in international organizations like the International Monetary Fund. Although the IMF once served the purpose of correcting short-term imbalances in international payments, it is now nothing short of a scandal. The IMF has actually contributed to economic crises in other countries.

The policy changes typically imposed by the IMF—devaluing currencies, raising taxes, cutting consumption—have only intensified the economic crises in countries such as Indonesia, Russia, South Korea, Thailand, and Brazil. The IMF has dampened promising export markets in economies it was supposedly trying to help. All told, this privileged bureaucracy has contributed to the impoverishment of huge numbers of people around the world.

The main beneficiaries of this highly secretive, highly bureaucratic organization have been large banks that have made risky loans at low interest rates, knowing that the IMF would bail them out if things went sour. This practice of socializing the risks of failed investments is often the very reason these economies find themselves in crisis.

The IMF has promoted policies that we would never put up with here in the United States. Even worse, it has done so with billions of U.S. taxpayer dollars, money that often evaporates almost instantly. The Russians admitted openly to lying to the IMF to win an infusion of nearly twenty billion dollars in aid and then defaulted on its foreign and bank debt soon after receiving the first installment. We would do much better by giving humanitarian aid and facilitating open markets and the rule of law in places like Russia and Indonesia rather than helping preserve inefficient state industries and promoting crushing tax increases that send struggling economies spiraling downward.

By failing to insist on reforms in IMF practices, the Clinton-Gore team has contributed to the most dangerous global financial and economic crisis since the 1930s. In 1997 and 1998, the formerly vibrant economies in Southeast Asia practically collapsed. Indonesia's gross domestic product, measured in U.S. dollars, shrank by an incredible 80 percent. The turmoil has been so intense that in some cases, the wages, pensions, and savings of almost an entire generation have been wiped out.

That is a horrendous record. We should insist that not a single dime of American money will flow into the IMF until and unless that organization undergoes fundamental change and begins opening the doors of opportunity for struggling nations instead of slamming them shut. We must insist on policies that are pro-freedom, pro-growth, and pro-entrepreneur.

LOOKING FORWARD

We need to build a fair, open, rules-based trade policy that expands international commerce and keeps America strong. We should restore presidential fast-track negotiating authority; expand NAFTA to include Chile and build a free-trade zone throughout the Americas; seek every opportunity to expand free-trade zones with allies and market economies such as the European Union, Australia, New Zealand, and Singapore; expand world trade rules to cover agriculture, services, and intellectual property more fully; build a worldwide free-trade zone for Internet commerce; enforce our trade laws to combat dumping and other unfair trade practices; reward reliable trading partners and democracies like Taiwan by promoting their entry into the World Trade Organization; end the anti-growth practices of the IMF; and promote market-oriented reforms, deregulation, and stable currencies in places such as China, Russia, Indonesia, Brazil, and even Japan.

America has nothing to fear from the global marketplace. Far from it. As the world's largest, freest, and most advanced economy, we are also the most competitive. We can maintain a clear-eyed defense of our own interests and, at the same time, lead the world in the direction of free and fair trade. By rising to these challenges and exporting our ideals to other nations, we can usher in a new era of prosperity and stability that brings new hope and opportunity to people around the world.

17

Preserving the American Advantage

A MERICA ENJOYS enormous advantages in the face of global challenges. Competition from abroad in the next decade may raise some novel questions, but our principles should not change: More freedom and greater economic growth remain the best hope for global progress. Competition spurs greater accomplishments.

But as much as we can and should be proud of our economic successes, it is also true that we could accomplish much more. Unfettered by government interference, the American spirit of innovation is easily the most powerful creative force in the world. What is amazing is that we have accomplished so much considering the layers upon layers of regulations the average business has to endure. It is a near miracle that we keep increasing productivity in a society that strangles many new ideas in the crib through the fear of liability and frivolous lawsuits.

Our present regulatory state and the litigation society have their proponents. Their arguments are focused on goals with which I have no quarrel: a cleaner, healthier environment; safer workplaces and products; justice for wrongs done to individuals. I do quarrel with their means of reaching these goals. We are undermining our economy's entrepreneurial and job-creating powers through excessive regulation, overzealous litigation, and radical environmentalism.

THE REGULATORY STATE

Last year, fifty-three departments and agencies of the federal government spent seventeen billion dollars writing new regulations and enforcing old ones. The *Code of Federal Regulations*, which collects all current regulations—in fine print, I might add—takes up 204 volumes and occupies nearly twenty feet of shelf space. And, though these regulations have the force of law, they have not been voted on by a single elected official. Winston Churchill once observed that "if you have ten thousand regulations you destroy all respect for the law." The federal bureaucracy added nearly five thousand new regulations in 1998 alone.

Perhaps you have managed to organize your life so that you are free from the impositions of this massive federal apparatus. Congratulations.

But you are still paying the price. Regulations are less visible than taxes, but they can prove equally burdensome. Federal regulations are estimated to cause a $1.3 trillion drag on the economy every year. An EPA-funded study estimated that in 1990 clean air and water regulations alone reduced America's gross national product by 6 percent. In fact, every American now spends more than forty days working just to pay for the cost of these federal regulations. Close to 20 percent of the average household's aftertax budget goes to meeting these regulatory costs.

Worried about paying for your kids' college education? According to Gerhard Casper, president of Stanford University, 7.5 cents of every tuition dollar at Stanford is a result of government regulations. He believes the indirect cost of complying with the array of regulations wastes another 5 cents of each tuition dollar.

We need to reform our regulatory system just as much as we need to overhaul the tax code. Silly, mindless, and outdated regulations abound. Many are incomprehensible. A Harvard University study estimated that federal regulations directly cost six hundred billion dollars to implement but provide only two hundred billion dollars in benefits to society.

I have consistently championed regulatory reform. When I served in the Senate, I posted on my office wall a 1971 article my grandfather had written entitled "Will the Federal Bureaucracy Destroy Individual Freedom in America?" as a reminder of what was at stake. When I served as vice president, I chaired the Council on Competitiveness, which fought ill-advised and counterproductive regulatory initiatives.

I took a lot of heat for that. But we had some important victories.

We succeeded in stopping a proposed Environmental Protection Agency rule that would have imposed one hundred million dollars in costs, with no likely effect on air pollution. We persuaded the Labor Department to eliminate its ban on work done at home by workers in the women's clothing industry. The council was also able to modify regulations proposed by the Department of Health and Human Services that would have required churches and other religious institutions offering day care to file detailed reports to the government. We oversaw the rewriting of the Federal Wetlands Manual after some bureaucrats had dramatically expanded the definition of "wetland" to include thousands of acres of dry land. Much of this land was productive Midwest farmland that I had walked on myself. By returning common sense to the process we were able to win a partial reprieve for the farmers and homeowners who were threatened by this bureaucratic power grab.

Here's what we need to do now:

Every significant regulatory proposal should be tested with a couple of common-sense questions. First, do the benefits of the proposed rule outweigh the cost, including the costs of lost jobs? Second, is the proposal based on sound science, with peer review by experts in the field, or is it merely something that sounds good and fits a preconceived theory?

Whenever proposals like these are advanced, the environmental zealots claim that the proposals are attempting to place a dollar value on human life. They are not. Rather, they reflect the simple truth that every law or regulation reflects a decision on where to devote society's scarce resources.

We have a number of quite serious environmental and health and safety challenges before us. But what is the priority? Common sense tells us that we should address the most serious risks or threats first. Do we do that now? No, we throw money and regulatory initiatives at everything. The result is that we can spend—as we have—more than ten billion dollars of scarce resources trying to clean up toxic waste sites with very little to show for it, while more serious risks and medical needs go unaddressed. A Harvard University dissertation in 1994 concluded that we lose sixty thousand lives per year because the government neglects to assess risks properly.

The regulatory process, moreover, imposes direct and indirect costs that cannot be justified.

First is the effect of lower economic growth and employment. The costs of complying with burdensome regulations have a negative effect on employment and wealth creation, thus harming human health and safety. As Supreme Court Justice Stephen Breyer notes in his recent book *Breaking the Vicious Cycle,* studies indicate that a 1 percent increase in unemployment is likely to cause an additional nineteen thousand heart attacks and perhaps result in more than a thousand suicides. As a result, many experts calculate that every seven million dollars spent to comply with regulations is likely to produce an additional death. That is a high cost to pay for a government regulation.

Second, proposed regulations sometimes create risks more severe than the ones they seek to remedy. For example, the Department of Energy estimated that EPA's proposal to reduce ozone levels would cause between 130 and 260 melanoma skin cancers per year and thousands of other cases of cancer and cataracts. I support requiring all federal agencies to minimize the net risks to our welfare.

One final philosophical point: Congress has to reassert its authority. There is no doubt that 535 legislators cannot—and should not—sit around and draft detailed regulations on a thousand subjects. But Congress has used this excuse to simply pass laws telling the executive branch to do this and that and let those bureaucrats figure it out. This is an abdication of its constitutional responsibility. Right now, the only way to correct a bad rule is for both houses of Congress to pass a law and for the president to sign it. In other words, a president can, by veto, easily stop such a "correction." And the veto will stand with the support of only one-third of either the House or the Senate. The unelected bureaucrats win. As economist William Niskanen has said, the "Constitution has been turned upside down."

Environmental Wisdom

I am committed to environmental stewardship in order to preserve the America we know for future generations. We have a moral imperative to leave the world cleaner than we found it. In the Book of Leviticus, God reminds us that the "land is mine" and we are "but aliens and sojourners" upon it.

I have hiked the Bob Marshall Mountains in Montana with my family, fly-fished the lakes and streams of Colorado and Wyoming, and spent nights under the stars in the Grand Canyon after days of rafting. These are among the many places I love in the great American outdoors. Along with millions of Americans I know firsthand how beautiful—how thrilling—is our inheritance of natural wonders. Places like these need protection. And since the days of Teddy Roosevelt, the Republican Party has embraced the conservation of natural resources as a key component of federal policy.

I have always supported environmental laws that wisely protect us from dangerous pollution and other real risks. But with all the progress we have made, the rhetoric of the environmentalists and their advocates like Al Gore have become shriller and more alarmist.

Such environmental alarmism threatens to undermine our freedom and to prevent many from achieving the American dream. Federal environmental laws take more than seventeen hundred pages just to print; another twelve thousand pages are needed to compile the official regulations. And EPA last year alone added more than ten thousand new pages. A respected Washington, D.C., think tank now estimates that by the year 2000 we will be spending more money on the environment than on national defense.

We are on the verge of making huge decisions with dramatic effects on our economy and our ability to create jobs—and the American people are cut out of the process. How? It is very simple.

Despite the widespread consensus in favor of environmental protection—witness twenty-five years of bipartisan laws on the subject—the environmental extremists have figured out that domestic support for radical and ill-conceived ideas is waning. So they have adopted a strategy of working through international institutions. Under this strategy, the executive branch can enter into agreements with other nations, and the agreements have the force of law without facing scrutiny by our elected representatives.

The Kyoto treaty on global warming is a prime example of environmental extremists using an international agreement to subvert the will of the American people. In this instance, Congress subsequently (and overwhelmingly) passed a resolution calling on Bill Clinton and Al Gore to submit this treaty for approval by the Senate, the process required by the Constitution. So far, they have refused to do so. Instead, the administration is spending time and energy trying to figure out how to implement this treaty and avoid such scrutiny.

This state of affairs must not be allowed to stand. The potential impact of the Kyoto treaty is startling. The Department of Energy estimates that the Kyoto treaty would reduce our GDP by 4 percent. The Department of Labor calculates that at least 1.2 million Americans will lose their jobs as a result. All for a theory that is the subject of significant dispute in the scientific community itself.

The Economist last year cast doubt on Al Gore's insistent claim that scientific opinion is "almost unanimously" in agreement on global warming by reprinting a 1975 *Newsweek* item reporting the "almost unanimous" scientific view that global *cooling* would "reduce agricultural productivity for the rest of the century." Gore's contribution to economic growth is evidenced by his fond hope, described in his book, *Earth in the Balance,* that the internal combustion engine would go the way of the dinosaurs. We need more sensible leadership than that.

We can protect the environment without sacrificing either our prosperity or our freedoms. We should encourage people to take personal responsibility for guarding the environment. We should seek incentives that prompt the development of better technology in the free market. It's a sure bet that the free market can accomplish precisely the same objective established by a government agency, but do so in a way that is vastly cheaper and more effective.

We must also protect private property rights. The worst polluters in the world were the former communist states that failed to recognize private property. An absence of ownership means an absence of accountability. But it is also true that accountability must extend to the government. The "inalienable" right to private property was so important that the Founding Fathers placed protections for it in the Third, Fourth, Fifth, and Seventh Amendments to the Constitution. The Fifth Amendment requires that private property shall not be taken for public use without "just compensation." In simple cases where government seeks to take private property outright, the rules and outcomes have long since been decided fairly. But in recent years, government has been exploiting its powers. Rather than physically taking the property, it instead adopts regulations that severely limit an owner's use of the property.

Any regulations that stop owners from exercising their property rights are "regulatory takings." If a regulation is important enough to adopt, the entire burden should not be visited on a single or a few property owners. If the benefits are to society as a whole, then society as a whole should be willing to pay the cost of taking the property.

That is my definition of "just."

LEASHING THE LAWYERS

Is there anyone who does not understand what the trial lawyers have inflicted on the middle class over the past two decades? Certainly the average American knows. That is why lawyers as a group are held in very low esteem—a sad indictment of a profession that is still full of many fine and dedicated men and women. More concretely, a respected consulting firm has calculated that our current tort system imposes $152 billion in direct costs on American families; the same firm estimates that the indirect costs top $300 billion (which doubled between the mid-1960s and the mid-1980s). More than 2 percent of our GDP is devoted to nothing but resolving disputes in our court system—five times greater than Great Britain and seven times greater than Japan.

That is a staggering price to pay for the leisure of the trial lawyers.

In my first campaign for Congress in 1976, as I was walking a precinct in New Haven, Indiana, I buttonholed a voter who asked if I was a lawyer. When I told him yes, he said, "Then I'll never vote for you." I countered that I wasn't actually practicing at the time, that I was in the newspaper business. He shot back, "Newspapers! That's even worse."

There is not much a president can do about journalists—and he would be a fool to try—but I certainly aim to do something about leashing the lawyers.

On August 13, 1991, I made my share of enemies among trial lawyers when I went before the American Bar Association—the largest voluntary professional association in the world—and laid out the case for legal reform. The statistics then, as now, showed a civil justice system that costs too much, takes too long to resolve disputes, and fails to provide enough alternatives to litigation. I told the assembled lawyers that our civil justice system had become a self-inflicted competitive disadvantage and that our profession had an obligation to lead the way in making common-sense reforms.

What happened next continues to astound me and should shock you: The president of the ABA charged onto the stage and denounced my remarks as a threat to justice in America.

Ordinary Americans, naturally, responded differently. I received letters by the bushel, running about a hundred to one in support of my statements.

Our country has fallen victim to a kind of litigation fever. Millions of new lawsuits are filed every year in the state and federal courts. The products Americans buy every day, from stepladders to prescription medications, carry a hidden surcharge: the cost of the legal battles that rage year in and year out. As much as 15 percent of the cost of pacemakers, 50 percent of the cost of football helmets, and 70 percent of the cost of childhood vaccines can be traced to the fear of liability and the expense of litigation.

This litigation explosion has already had a particularly destructive impact on healthcare in this country. A Stanford University study estimates the annual cost at fifty billion dollars. There were more medical malpractice suits filed between 1977 and 1987 than in all prior years of U.S. history combined. Annual malpractice premiums exceed six billion dollars. The cost of defensive medicine — tests or procedures performed for the purpose of avoiding litigation — is estimated to cost another twenty-five billion annually.

It should be no surprise that the costs of healthcare rise as a result.

In testimony before Congress, a small-business owner from Harrisburg, Pennsylvania, pointed out that his family-owned company, now 155 years old, was never sued in its first 130 years of operation. But in the last quarter-century it has been sued fourteen times. This litigation has meant spending "thousands of hours and tens of thousands of dollars responding to suits and collecting the information to exonerate ourselves." In addition, the business owner's yearly insurance bill has gone from several hundred dollars in the 1970s to more than forty thousand dollars in the 1990s.

Even the Girl Scouts are not immune. Several years ago, it was reported that the cost of liability insurance for the Girl Scouts required the sale of eighty thousand boxes of their cookies.

Aside from shackling innovation and hurting competitiveness, litigation fever harms our culture. When courts become clogged and those with genuine disputes must sacrifice huge amounts of time and money to get their day in court, access to justice is actually reduced. Judge Learned Hand, one of the great jurists of the twentieth century, said he dreaded involvement in a lawsuit "more than anything short of sickness and death." Most people who have ever been parties to litigation feel the same way. In today's litigating culture, people who have done nothing wrong can be dragged into court by plaintiffs who are either trying to pin responsibility for their own actions on someone else, or trying to cash in on the lawsuit lottery. Innocence is no guarantee against harassment by lawsuits and the risk of financial ruin.

Sometimes you simply cannot escape liability, no matter how hard you twist and turn. The school board members of Francis Scott Key High School in Maryland were afraid that if they didn't field a female running back on the football team they would be subject to a major lawsuit. She was tackled during the first play of her first scrimmage and was seriously hurt. Years later she filed a lawsuit against the board of education for $1.5 million on the grounds that no one had explained to her "the potential risk of serious and disabling injury inherent in the sport."

In California, the parents of a child who had threatened to kill fellow students sued when the child was suspended. They won an award from the U.S. Circuit Court of Appeals for private-school tuition and $360,000 in legal fees.

The more we encourage litigation, the more we encourage a mind-set that destroys friendships, fractures business relationships, and breeds mistrust.

We also undermine our right to self-government. As writer Jonathan Rauch has noted, the actions of plaintiffs' trial lawyers have created a growing web of "intricate social regulation that enfolds even the most minute details of everyday life." As a result of thousands of lawsuits, government has come to regulate such areas as "whom you can date at work, what jokes you can tell, even the rules of professional golf."

We may or may not agree on the individual results in thousands of cases brought all over the country. But we should all agree that social policy should be fashioned by voters and their accountable representatives, not by lawyers.

In 1997 and 1998, eighteen different states enacted some form of liability reform legislation, so the ball is clearly rolling in the right direction. Iowa has enacted a comprehensive tort-reform package that made significant progress on a number of fronts, including such intricate issues as damage calculation. I support these reforms.

I also support state actions to place reasonable limits on awards for punitive damages and reform the rules of "joint and several liability" to ensure that only those truly responsible for injuries are required to pay for them. We must achieve a dramatic reduction in the number of frivolous cases brought in America's courts. The best way of doing so is to experiment with what I term a "fairness rule" in disputes arising under state law but brought for resolution to the federal courts. The rule would require the loser of the lawsuit to pay the winner's legal fees.

We also need to curb the proliferation of class action suits. Class action suits have served as a license for lawyers to extort money from successful businesses without obtaining much compensation for their "clients." You may have been lucky enough in 1995 to get a couple of coupons in the mail for a discount of ten dollars or so on airline tickets. The lawyers got $14.4 million for their effort in settling that class action suit against nine airlines. In another class action suit, filed against Packard Bell, the lawyers objected to new computers containing some recycled parts. The case settled in two months; the lawyers received about four million dollars in exchange for Packard Bell's agreement to note in future instruction manuals that their computers "may contain reconditioned parts." One judge remarked that the "modern equivalent" of "the roving bands of mercenaries who pillaged and robbed" and "nearly brought [Europe] to its knees" during the Hundred Years' War "is the plaintiff's attorney in . . . class actions."

Although my speech to the ABA was received coolly by the group's leadership, I was pleased to discover that most lawyers actually agreed with my assessment of the problems facing the legal system. Nevertheless, it's clear that a sizable group of trial lawyers is unalterably opposed to reforming the system that has made them wealthy. And it is also clear that they will continue to target for defeat anyone who has the temerity to rein them in.

But it needs to be done. For the sake of freedom, we must restore the legal system to its true purpose: the righting of wrongs and the prompt resolution of disputes.

18

Promoting the
American Advantage

F OR ALL THE unnecessary burdens imposed by government, the American economy is an extraordinary engine of growth and progress. In literally hundreds of ways, American businesses large and small are leading the world. Several sectors, however, are especially important to our overall economic well-being. The information-technology revolution, which has powered the breathtaking growth of the nineties, needs still further encouragement. Our space program, which has been a source of innovation and inspiration for decades, must continue to be fueled by a vision of American preeminence in every aspect of space science and exploration. And the farm economy, on which America's independence has depended for more than two hundred years, deserves a higher priority on the national agenda.

THE INFORMATION-TECHNOLOGY FRONTIER

Economist Larry Kudlow sums up perfectly the economic transformation of the last fifteen years: "The 1980s witnessed a technology surge, based mainly on advanced computer chips, cellular telephones and personal computers. In the 1990s all this was improved, but the big push has come from innovative and user-friendly software and Internet commerce."

On the eve of the twenty-first century, there are three things we must do immediately to preserve the information-technology sector on its remarkable trajectory of growth.

End the Antitrust Assault on American Success

The ideologically driven Clinton-Gore Department of Justice has apparently decided that its place in history depends upon distorting the meaning and purpose of the antitrust laws. Although we've been told that the era of big government is over, the antitrust division is still trying to grow, and the number of antitrust investigations is three times higher today than it was in 1989. In my travels across this country, no one—not a single person—has ever asked me to help halt the Microsoft menace. Americans intuitively understand the difference between competition and monopoly, and they don't see a monopoly in Microsoft. What they do see is an aggressive band of reputation-driven lawyers attacking success and, in the process, endangering a great American success story. It may be that the future will find a Microsoft, an America Online, an Intel, or some other high-tech titan alone atop the technology mountain, but the incredibly dynamic and competitive experience of Silicon Valley suggests otherwise. American antitrust enforcers have to stop their aggressive pursuit of headlines and return to the aggressive pursuit of genuine monopolies that are truly stifling business creation and injuring the interests of American consumers.

A Permanent Ban on Internet Taxation

Internet sales revenues were projected in the range of six to eight billion dollars in 1998. The actual numbers easily doubled the lower end of that range and may have topped thirteen billion dollars. Why this huge growth? Look in no small part to the Congress and its move last year to pass the Internet Tax Freedom Act, which put into place a three-year moratorium on new taxes on Internet commerce and Internet access. This new means of commerce rewards efficiency and benefits consumers by making available a world of shopping opportunities not even remotely matched by the largest shopping mall. As more people use the Internet—only one quarter of Americans now use it at all, much less shop on it—the prospects for online commerce seem limitless.

But that growth and its corresponding benefits for consumers, investors, and entrepreneurs could be throttled by a grab for tax revenues by state governments, or even by the federal government.

The three-year moratorium must be made a permanent fixture of federal tax policy, and the ban on state and local raids on Internet commerce should be made permanent. Not only will this protect the new marketplace, it will also encourage the states to focus on realistic revenue sources for the next century.

Visas for Talent

Immigration issues are among the most controversial in our country. I dealt with most of them in an earlier chapter. But one aspect of this issue involves the availability of visas for specially skilled high-tech workers from around the globe. The world's brightest minds will come to America—if we let them. And we should.

If we want to maintain our economic edge, we need the best talent we can find. I refuse to believe that there is a danger that

American companies will under-employ American talent if such talent is available. On the other hand, the high-tech environment is a ruthless respecter of ability. If that ability is to be found abroad, it should be welcomed here to help in the work of anchoring a general American prosperity in the next century.

LEADERSHIP IN SPACE

American preeminence in space science and exploration has shaped our everyday lives in ways we sometimes fail to appreciate. The space program has promoted the development of new medical devices, energy-storage systems, night-vision cameras, and a host of advances in communications technology. Satellites provide regular data on the condition of Earth's atmosphere and oceans. The weightless environment of space lets scientists conduct experiments that are impossible on Earth, holding out hope of finding new insights into diseases and the workings of the human body. Space-based systems are also a critical element of military communications, ship and aircraft navigation, and intelligence operations.

The space program captures headlines only sporadically, with newsmaking events such as the first photos from *Mars Pathfinder* or John Glenn's return to space. Hidden from regular view are the extraordinary day-to-day efforts that make American leadership possible.

When I became chairman of the National Space Council a decade ago, the space program had lost much of the luster it had acquired during the heyday of space exploration in the 1960s. Whereas the mere mention of NASA had once conjured up heroic, soul-stirring images in people's minds, lately it had become a lethargic bureaucracy that was regarded, one observer said, as "synonymous with institutional decay." Embarrassing mega-failures like the optical flaw in the Hubble telescope, the grounding of the space shuttle fleet due to unexplained gas leaks, and the failure of the billion-dollar *Mars '98 Observer* to hit its target all damaged NASA's reputation and weakened its hold on the imagination of the American people.

I'm proud to say we changed that, and working with Dr. Mark Albrecht, who was my choice to serve as the council's executive director, we installed new leadership at NASA that has continued to this day. (The man we selected to be its administrator, Dan Goldin, did such a fine job that he was retained in office by Bill Clinton.) We trimmed the agency's bureaucracy and instituted a new policy of "faster, cheaper, better" for NASA projects. We set in motion some of the initiatives that would make news years later, including the *Mars Pathfinder* mission and the space shuttle linkup with the Russian space station *Mir*. The international space station, which we rescued from Democrats in Congress who wanted to kill it, is now being assembled by an international team that includes American astronauts and Russian cosmonauts. NASA is once again a proud and pacesetting center of science and exploration.

Our future activities in space should follow this visionary path. The United States should boldly pursue control of space as a national objective. No other nation has the will, the know-how, and the credibility to lead the world in cooperative efforts like the space station. Further, we need to realize that some countries are likely to pursue space programs with unfriendly aims. Our technological leadership, therefore, is also a matter of national security.

Finally, I am committed to continued human exploration of space. Ten years ago, we set the goal of putting an astronaut on Mars by July 20, 2019, the fiftieth anniversary of Neil Armstrong's historic walk on the moon. It's impossible to predict what benefits—economic, medical, scientific, or otherwise—will emerge from a mission to Mars. But as President Kennedy recognized, Americans welcome the challenges of space exploration, "not because they are easy, but because they are hard."

AGRICULTURE IN THE TWENTY-FIRST CENTURY

We have become so accustomed to the abundance of our land that we now take for granted supermarkets the size of football fields. America's farmers have always been the backbone of our independence because no nation in the world could hold us hostage by threatening our supply of food. But today, while no foreign power can threaten America's agricultural economy, the shortsighted mistreatment of our farm communities could.

Growing up as the son of a newspaperman in the farming community of Huntington, Indiana, I learned that when farms prosper, so does Main Street. What was true of Huntington is true of the nation. About seventy-seven cents of every dollar spent on food and fiber in this country goes outside agriculture to the processing, marketing, transporting, and retailing industries. In all, about twenty-two million Americans' jobs rely on farm production. That's almost five jobs for every farmer. U.S. farm exports alone create more than a hundred billion dollars in economic activity in the United States and support almost one million jobs.

For the good of American agriculture and the American economy, we must return to the principles that guided the first Republican president, Abraham Lincoln, who started out in life on a farm. Lincoln's philosophy was simple: The federal government's role should be to help farmers and ranchers do what they do best, namely, produce food and fiber. Toward that end, he established the land-grant college system and the Homestead Act, and he created the United States Department of Agriculture to support research into better seeds and better farming practices. That same complex of research, education, and property rights must undergird our farm policy today and into the twenty-first century.

Unfortunately, as we prepare for a new century, American agriculture has still not shaken itself free of the pernicious effects of more than six decades of supply control, federal mandates, and production caps put in place in 1933 by President Franklin D. Roosevelt. FDR said at the time that his policies were meant to be only temporary. Sadly, however, those policies, in place for more than sixty years, have left a devastating economic legacy for rural America.

Federal supply-control programs clearly have been a net financial drain on America's farmers, especially over the last two decades. For example, over the life of the 1981, 1990, and 1995 farm bills, farm payments averaged $17 billion per year. In order to receive these payments, however, farmers were required to idle significant portions of their land—a requirement that, according to the Hudson Institute's Center for Global Food Issues, cost America's cotton, wheat, and feed grain farmers between $25 billion and $45 billion in revenue per year. In short, farm programs have cost farmers more than $250 billion in forgone income.

The number one issue for farmers and ranchers today is risk management. Democrats in Congress have called for more federal supply-control programs to address low commodity prices, but that would only turn back the clock on farm policy. Taking more acres of farmland out of production would simply encourage greater farm production by our competitors in Latin America and Europe. The Clinton-Gore administration has promised crop insurance and risk management reforms for three years but has not kept its promises. Those reforms are needed now.

The overall challenge for farm policy in the twenty-first century will be to ensure a prosperous future for farming through a combination of more trade, new technology, and lower taxes.

More Trade

Sen. Pat Roberts of Kansas calls opening markets through trade negotiations the "other side of the ledger sheet" when it comes to the Freedom to Farm reform passed in 1996. He's right that cutting farm spending and throwing out the counterproductive rules that go with supply control is only half the job. The government's role now should be to open new export markets for agriculture—a task at which the Clinton-Gore administration has failed miserably.

The bottom line is that U.S. farmers are still shut out of many markets. Our exports face high tariffs or outright bans or bogus health claims. The European Union keeps out our meat by means of their scientifically discredited hormone ban. They also set illegitimate, unwarranted barriers to our soybeans with their rules on genetically modified organisms. Even beyond these protectionist hurdles, however, U.S. farmers face an increasing number of impediments ranging from document requirements to procedural delays to illogical regulations. As a result of these and other problems, U.S. exports of agricultural products have dropped 16 percent since peaking in 1996.

Unfortunately, not all the hurdles faced by America's agricultural exporters come from our trading partners; sometimes they come from our own government. The most disastrous case, of course, remains the Jimmy Carter grain embargo in 1980. At the time, the Soviet Union represented about 10 percent of the market for our wheat exports. And ironically, U.S. wheat farmers are still locked out of more than 10 percent of the world wheat market because of U.S.-imposed sanctions on other nations. As we learned in 1980, unilateral sanctions rarely have the effect they are intended to. Frequently they backfire.

Senate Agriculture Committee chairman Richard Lugar has proposed a comprehensive approach to unilateral U.S. economic sanctions. I share his belief that the decision to impose sanctions must involve an evaluation of domestic economic costs, foreign policy costs, and humanitarian consequences as well as the likely impact on U.S. agriculture—especially its consequences on the U.S. record as a reliable supplier.

New Technology

Agriculture has been a leader at adapting technology, especially technology that preserves and benefits the environment. For example, California farmers now use less water for irrigation than they did thirty years ago, yet they are producing 60 percent more food. Likewise, across the Midwest and South, farmers are using conservation tillage to cut soil erosion by 90 percent and to protect surface waters from runoff.

The key to meeting the environmental challenges that face agriculture lies in putting new technology into the hands of those who care most about the land—those who make a living from it. Local watershed problems won't be solved by bureaucrats in Brussels or Geneva or, for that matter, in Washington, D.C. Farmers have adopted new technologies that have reduced runoff, soil erosion, and other problems because it made sense to their pocketbooks to do so and because they love the land and the resources they steward.

Given this example, my plan is based on a common-sense idea: that the environment will not be preserved without working with the landowners and others who manage it. Punitive, excessive regulations on farmers won't help the environment. Assistance and cooperation with them will. Too many farmers and ranchers are faced with being put out of business by environmental penalties and fines even if they voluntarily come forward in good faith to ask for assistance in correcting environmental problems. That must stop. To preserve the environment and maintain a profitable role for U.S. agriculture through technology, we must maintain our commitment to agricultural research—private as well as public—and extend immunity to farmers who, in good faith, conduct environmental assessments of their operations to determine where new technologies may help correct areas that are not in compliance with current environmental laws or standards.

Finally, we must streamline the approval process for biotech products. Biotechnology has the potential of engineering the toxicity out of livestock manure or developing drought-resistant or virus-resistant crops. Overregulation in this field could drive our livestock-feeding industry to Latin America. Biotech is becoming the cutting edge of farm productivity, and it holds the promise of healthier, richer life for all mankind.

Lower Taxes

Like most American small businesses, farmers and ranchers are overtaxed, especially when it comes to capital gains and estate taxes.

Capital gains taxes fall especially hard on farmers. Because farmland is held, on average, more than twenty-eight years, nearly three decades of inflation are taxed when it is sold. In fact, some farmers and ranchers can be faced with a tax bill that is more than twice the real, inflation-adjusted capital gain on their land. Thus, farmers and ranchers who have held and invested in their land all their careers suffer serious harm. For most of them, their land is their retirement plan. They intend to sell it to a son or daughter when they retire, but punitive capital gains taxes force them to stay active in the farm. Indeed, approximately 40 percent of all farmers are age fifty-five or older. This has a twofold effect on the agricultural economy. First, in the short run it forces two generations to share income from a single farm, making it financially tough on both. Second, over the longer run it prevents younger farmers from getting started, investing in new technology, and spreading out their investments over a longer period.

The problems caused by high capital gains tax rates are compounded by high estate tax rates. The "death tax," like the capital gains tax, falls heavily on farmers and their highly visible fixed assets of land and buildings. It wreaks havoc on rural communities. Large corporations and chain stores don't have to contend with estate taxes, but farms, ranches, and the kind of small businesses that build communities do. Indeed, death taxes often force farms to be broken up or sold off—especially those farms that, because of high capital gains taxes, have had to support two generations of families.

I have laid out my tax proposals earlier in this book, but it is worth reemphasizing that the current system is badly injuring our farm sector. We need quick action to end this inequitable burden on the industry that literally puts bread on our tables.

The Focus on Farming

I know that farm policy may weary readers who are unfamiliar with its technical jargon. But we cannot expect the middle class to prosper in the face of a dwindling farm sector. If we are going to seriously address the needs of the middle class, we have to focus on farm policy for the long term and not treat it as a topic for presidential attention only in the months before the Iowa caucuses.

PART 5

Security Abroad

Foreign policy must be clear, consistent, and confident.

— DWIGHT D. EISENHOWER

19

Opportunities Squandered

Are you better off now than you were four years ago?" Ronald Reagan asked the American people when he ran for president against Jimmy Carter in 1980. This year and in 2000, I also intend to place a question before the American people: "Is our nation more secure today than it was eight years ago?"

In 1992, America stood at the peak of global power and influence. Communism had been cast aside in Eastern Europe and Russia with hardly a shot being fired, and its resurgence seemed impossible. The regional influence of Iraq's Saddam Hussein had been terminated by U.S. forces in the most lopsided military victory of modern times. America's armed forces stood proudly in a high state of morale and readiness—well-equipped, well-funded, and engaged in cutting-edge research and development. America was able and willing to defend its economic interests—our investments, markets, and resource supplies—in key regions of the globe, often as the leader of powerful alliances. The United States's role as an example and as a defender of democracy, free markets, and human rights was asserted and generally welcomed in the Americas, Asia, Europe, and even in the Middle East. Nations that might have challenged the value system that made this "the American century" lay low.

None of those statements holds true today. Bill Clinton and Al Gore have not "pursued" a foreign policy in any meaningful sense. Foreign policy has pursued them. The past six-plus years have been characterized by a series of improvisations best described as petulance toward some and posturing toward others. Our government has lost the courage to lead. It has been hostile to friends such as Israel, embarrassed by small-time thugs in places such as North Korea and Iraq, and intimidated by serious global players like China and Russia. Our national defense has eroded so far that our exposure to missile attack is no longer simply limited to Russia and China but will soon include North Korea and others.

And even in this era of global terrorism—the bombings of our embassies in Kenya and Tanzania and the destruction of our barracks in Saudi Arabia—the Clinton-Gore administration devotes vastly more time and attention to the theoretical threat of global warming than to the very real threat of global terrorism.

Our country's present foreign and military strategy wavers between bluster and slickness—empty of strategic thought, full of vacillation. Shockingly, we appear to have the first poll-driven foreign policy in history. We have squandered many opportunities, and we have forfeited many advantages.

It's More Than "The Economy, Stupid"

"It's the economy, stupid," we were told by the Clinton campaign in 1992. We now know what Bill Clinton, Al Gore, and many other

American politicians really meant by that: If there's no current crisis in the world, don't waste your time reflecting on foreign policy and the true basis of American security and prosperity. Follow the polls. Just keep the world at bay until after the next election. Buy time. Squander our American inheritance.

This is a dangerous, self-fulfilling cycle, and by no means is it leadership. When candidates for office and top elected officials avoid debate on foreign policy and national security, then the American people tend to ignore those vital topics. Public indifference is reflected in the polls. Politicians read the polls. And the vicious cycle starts all over again. America's loyal soldiers watch this cycle with sadness, and America's enemies observe it with glee.

I will break the cycle. I will engage the American people in a long-overdue discussion concerning our national security and the means of protecting it. Foreign policy must be at the center of debate in a presidential campaign. It is the duty of leaders to alert the American people to the dangers in the world. The country cannot afford another presidential election that treats international security issues as the exclusive domain of policy wonks and editorial writers. The next president must not be someone in need of on-the-job training. In 2000, no presidential candidate should be taken seriously unless he or she understands the importance of this agenda and has the credentials and experience to guide America through what will be very perilous years.

BEYOND THE IN-BOX FOREIGN POLICY

I will start by making clear my general beliefs about U.S. foreign policy—the doctrine I will follow as president and commander in chief. Without a doctrine, and without a strategy for navigating the numerous demands on U.S. power, our nation's diplomats and soldiers become captives of the in-box.

Mistakes in domestic policy can be costly, but with the right policies they can be easily remedied. Mistakes in foreign policy are something else: They waste lives and can take generations to repair. We continue, for example, to live with the consequences of the failed LBJ-McNamara "no-win" policy in Vietnam nearly three decades after the war ended. The country, and for that matter the world, cannot afford another four years of improvisation in the face of multiplying international crises.

The way to avoid improvisation is for a president to formulate and articulate clear principles that guide U.S. foreign policy—not for every circumstance, of course, but for most circumstances. The Clinton-Gore administration never did that. I will.

ISOLATIONISM VERSUS INTERNATIONALISM: A FALSE CHOICE

Pundits would have us believe that there are two schools of thought on foreign policy in the Republican Party, the isolationist school and the internationalist school. Frankly, those labels tell us very little. Pat Buchanan, for example, is not a head-in-the-sand isolationist, though he is often portrayed that way. And Republican advocates of energetic American engagement do not display the reflexive submission to international opinion that characterizes the Clinton-Gore administration. In any event, I have never placed myself on one side or the other of that false divide.

The so-called "isolationists" who call for American retrenchment from international obligations are emphatically right when they reject the way today's liberals, with their 1960s distaste for the armed forces, want to treat the American military as an international police force. They are right to distinguish the defense of our national security from adventures like the occupation of Haiti.

They are also right in their skepticism about the stream of treaties and covenants that are regularly churned out by various international organizations without consultation with America's elected leaders. They are right to question the drift toward subordination of U.S. national interests to the collective—I might say, collectivist—opinion of other governments. Perhaps most importantly, they are right when they oppose the presidential commitment of American troops in situations that don't demand it.

They are wrong, however, when their eagerness to avoid foreign entanglements leads to proposals that would destabilize critical areas and invite aggression. It's one thing to question whether we need to maintain every single military base in the world. After all, times and technology do change, and our defense posture must change accordingly. It's quite another thing to suggest a lessening of the U.S. troop commitment in Korea, given the instability that prevails north of the thirty-eighth parallel.

Meanwhile, I sympathize with many of the "internationalist" points of view. The American people sacrificed, suffered, and spent too much in the defeat of Nazism and communism to walk away now from world leadership. Our nation's foreign policy has always had a strong moral component. It has never been based exclusively on cold political calculation. Nor should it be now, when humanitarian considerations call for our active engagement against persecution and genocide.

But the internationalist perspective can also be taken to extremes, as when it fails to distinguish between the emergency use of our armed forces to facilitate an international humanitarian mission (the way President Bush acted in Somalia) and the longer-term exposure of those forces to the savagery of a civil war (the way President Clinton acted in Somalia). My internationalist Republican friends err when they expect the United States to be an active party in virtually every international rescue mission. Clearly, some situations are more threatening to our national interest—and to world peace—than others. But it is a rare local conflict that cannot be better handled through regional action.

A New Doctrine

My approach is to put aside the one-word labels and to revise the doctrines that guided American foreign policy in earlier generations. There are times, Lincoln said, when "the dogmas of the quiet past are inadequate to the stormy present."

The most important question, of course, has to be the role of America in the post–Cold War world. This is a more complex issue than might appear to be the case. For example, the foreign policy establishment has recently embraced the idea that, as the world's only superpower, America can show "leadership" only by using the American military. But it is fundamentally wrong to assume that this is always true. We should be wise enough in the exercise of our military power that the rest of the world will call upon it only rarely, when our vital national interests are at stake.

In most cases, America's greatest contribution as the world's only superpower is to serve as the one honest broker on whom every other nation can rely to help resolve conflicts. Our policy concerning Kosovo may have begun with that intent, but we stumbled badly by making ourselves a party to a civil war. Simply stated, this is the wrong war in the wrong place.

American foreign policy has been most successful when guided by clear principles—from the Monroe Doctrine to the Reagan Doctrine, which promised support for freedom fighters facing Soviet-backed regimes. As Kosovo makes clear, we have at present no such clear framework, no principles guiding the use of our military. I believe five key principles apply.

1. Defense of the American homeland is the vital national interest. This seems obvious, but in fact, our priorities today do not reflect this simple principle. The United States must field a well-trained and well-equipped military capable of protecting our country from all external threats, including the threat of ballistic-missile attack, the threat of terrorism, and the threat posed by weapons of mass destruction. Yet with each crisis du jour, we continue to send our troops and our ships to every imaginable "hot spot" while we wear out the troops, sacrifice our readiness, and deplete our stocks.

2. Protecting the Americas. The Americas, especially Central America and the Caribbean, will always be the next most important strategic area of interest to us. Whether it is the threat of communist rule over the last forty years or the direct effect of instability in this region, the United States has always responded more forcefully here than would be appropriate in other regions of the world. Whether it was Panama or Grenada, supporting the contras or enforcing the embargo against Cuba, we have by our actions made clear—appropriately so—that a peaceful, democratic, and prosperous North, Central, and South America is our chief foreign policy priority.

3. Engagement abroad to protect vital U.S. interests. The United States must be prepared to fulfill its alliance commitments, to defend its essential economic interests anywhere in the world, and to prevent the rise of another military power capable of challenging the United States on a large scale. This still requires a U.S. military presence in Asia and in Europe as insurance against the possibility of the rise of a dominating and aggressive power, and will require an unwavering commitment to the security of Israel.

Where civil war occurs in a region in which the United States has a strategic interest, we must, of course, consider the potential that the conflict will spread. Still, we must insist that regional powers take the lead or they will always assume we will do so for them. The fact that we are part of NATO does not—and should not—automatically bring with it an obligation to be involved in every European crisis. And we should never allow alliances like NATO—which are held together by our leadership—to dictate the agenda to us.

4. *Support for democracy and human rights.* In some conflicts, our natural role as an honest broker may yield to our traditional support for those who fight for democracy and human rights. This properly occurred when we backed freedom fighters against Soviet-sponsored aggression. And it may be appropriate in circumstances where peace and a just resolution of the issues is nearly impossible. But it does not necessarily require American troops. We can pro-vide material aid and, if need be, military supplies to groups fighting against brutal oppression—in Sudan, for example, where slavery on a mass scale and hundreds of thousands of deaths of Christians seem to have escaped notice in Washington, D.C. But however frustrating it is, we must also recognize that in some cases there will be little we can do. It is a sad truth that atrocities occur on every side of some conflicts.

Just as important as our military might is the power of our ideas. Not every conflict is economic in origin, but it is usually the case that age-old hatreds explode in times of want, hunger, and distress. We need to keep our eye on promoting global peace and prosperity. That means stopping the IMF from inflicting misery on entire nations and instead exporting the ideas that we know work: the rule of law, free elections, free markets, low tax rates, and stable cur-rencies. This too is real leadership.

5. *American credibility.* We should never confuse our credibility with the credibility of NATO or the United Nations. Our role as the world's only superpower extends well beyond Europe; if we get

it wrong there, we risk more crises in other parts of the world. This is the essential difference between the United States and every other member of NATO.

The framework I propose will not make every future decision easy. It does, however, establish a pattern for decisions that is quite obviously lacking today.

20

Running on Empty

O N FEBRUARY 24, 1991, American-led coalition forces
launched an all-out attack to expel Iraqi divisions from their
positions in occupied Kuwait. One hundred hours later, Iraqi
forces surrendered, completely defeated in one of the most one-
sided military victories the world has ever witnessed. America's
armed forces were arguably the best equipped, best trained, and
most effective forces ever fielded. Now, after years of defense cuts,
we hear stories reminiscent of the 1970s—of a "hollow army" expe-
riencing difficulty in recruiting and retaining quality personnel; of
planes that can't fly for lack of spare parts; and of low morale
resulting from pay gaps, reduced retirement benefits, and an operations tempo higher than it was at the height of the Cold War.

If the United States had to fight the Persian Gulf War again, it could not do so without exposing itself to significant risks in other parts of the world. Incredible as it may sound, to conduct the Persian Gulf deployment today would require two-thirds of the army, two-thirds of our aircraft carriers, two-thirds of our air force wings, and 100 percent of the marine corps' fighting strength.

America's military capabilities also have not kept pace with the emergence of new threats posed by rogue groups or nations with weapons of mass destruction—chemical, nuclear, and biological weapons—and long-range missile systems to deliver those weapons. Over the next several years, not only will these weapons threaten the survival of our friends and allies in the Middle East, Europe, and Asia, but they will also present serious challenges to our ability to project American power to these regions to defend our friends and protect our interests. In the not too distant future, the American homeland itself will be at risk from missile attack, not just by other global powers that can be deterred by the threat of nuclear retaliation, but by rogue groups or nations who may not be deterred by such a threat.

Finally, we have clear indications that future wars will be quite different from what we experienced in Operation Desert Storm. It is unlikely that any future enemy will give us six months to build up our forces, and it is increasingly difficult to maintain overseas forces and bases during peacetime. As a result, new ways of projecting power from the United States homeland will become crucial to military success. The opportunities offered by the information revolution, along with long-range precision strike capabilities and advances in space technology, all make clear that there is an emerging revolution in military affairs. There will be a fundamental change in the way wars are fought. But America now spends virtually nothing on research and development of the technologies and techniques that would continue to make the nation's armed forces second to none.

A DEPLETED FORCE

The readiness problems of the 1990s are of an entirely new character. We do not have a hollow force like that of the 1970s. We have today a *depleted* force. History's most effective fighting force, painstakingly rebuilt during the twenty years following the end of the Vietnam War, has been almost completely exhausted. There has been no effective replenishment since 1991, and there is little on the horizon. Across all the armed services, the Clinton-Gore administration has been cutting into our military's reserves while refusing the critical resupply of men and machines that is necessary.

For example, air power has always been an American competitive advantage. Until now, American pilots and the planes they fly have been unmatched. Today, however, the United States is suffering a serious shortage of combat pilots. In 1996, the air force lost five hundred pilots to civilian life. By the end of 1998, it was nearly seven hundred pilots short. Back in 1981, when trained air force pilots were offered a large bonus for committing themselves to serving for an additional five years, 81 percent of those eligible accepted. In 1997, the rate was down to 59 percent, and in 1998 it dropped to less than 30 percent. Only 10 percent of the navy's qualified pilots accepted their proposed bonus. The navy is now short of its needs by 40 percent.

The navy also ended 1998 some seven thousand sailors short of its recruiting target, leaving it short overall by twenty-two thousand sailors. The master chief aboard the USS *Enterprise* reported in 1997 that his senior noncommissioned officers were not staying on to retirement; instead, they were leaving the service after sixteen or seventeen years. These men are the core of our navy.

When the USS *George Washington* sailed into the Persian Gulf in 1996 for another confrontation with Saddam Hussein, it had 5,500 sailors aboard; a year later it had only 4,655. These shortages mean that crews have to put in longer shifts and make up work outside their specialties in places such as the ammunition magazines, which demand mostly muscle and endurance. The ship's executive officer said the shortages "probably added two to three hours to a workday that was already thirteen hours long."

Indeed, the navy is probably the service most affected by the depletion of our military forces in the 1990s. In the ninety-six months from 1990 through 1997, the navy was called to respond to ninety-three contingencies. But ships are increasingly unfit for combat, aircraft are showing the signs of age and wear, sailors are leaving in droves, and new recruitment is way down.

Even the navy's shore facilities are exhibiting the service's readiness problems. The chief of naval operations (CNO) reported in October 1998 that in "some hangars, the roof leaks so badly that water damage to aircraft is a serious threat." The CNO also reported that some critical munitions are beginning to come up on shortage lists, especially the Tomahawk Block II cruise missile, the weapon of choice since the Persian Gulf War. Because of ammunition shortages for training in the March 1998 deployment to the Persian Gulf, the strike squadron aboard the USS *Abraham Lincoln* had only one pilot who had ever flown from a carrier and delivered a laser-guided bomb. The CNO told the Senate, "A decade ago, 70 percent of the Navy's non-deployed units were at the highest readiness levels. . . . Today barely half are that ready." In March 1997, the House National Security Committee reported that only forty-four of seventy-six aircraft belonging to one of the navy's carrier air wings were in flying condition, largely due to shortages of spare parts. "The United States military has been living off the assets it bought in the 1980s (or even earlier)," former undersecretary of state Robert Zoellick told the Senate Budget Committee last February. "The 'procurement holiday' of the 1990s will leave America with a bad hangover."

CRISIS IN CONFIDENCE

In addition to shortages of men and materiel, there has been a sharp drop of confidence in their leadership among soldiers, sailors, airmen, and marines. This crisis of confidence has even led some military officers to openly criticize the moral character of the commander in chief, which is potentially an offense warranting court-martial.

We must restore the morale of our armed forces by recognizing that respect is a two-way street. I'm greatly concerned with the consistent lack of respect for the military exhibited by this administration. I'm also concerned with some of the recent movements toward "closing the gap" between military and civilian culture through a variety of means ranging from softer codes of conduct and "sensitivity training" to ill-advised gender integration in basic training. The military exists to defend our freedom, not to serve as a laboratory for social experiments proposed by political activists who are hostile to the military culture. As John Hillen of the Center for Strategic and International Studies has said,

> [I]f the end-state of having a military is to provide for the common defense of the nation, to include the rather arduous task of fighting and winning wars, then we might not want the military to look too much like a society that produces magazine covers like "The Ten Commandments: What They Mean Now." Contrary to some conventional wisdom, peacekeeping is not likely to be the only military mission of the future, and advanced technology is not likely to land every GI in an air-conditioned trailer. War will be the hell it has always been, warriors will be needed to fight it, and a military culture that produces them should stand up and defend the ethos that allows it to do just that.

It's also time to realize that members of our shrinking military have been run ragged in recent years. During the past eight years we have deployed our forces around the globe thirty-eight times, almost four times more often than during the previous thirty years. At any given time, more than half the U.S. Navy is at sea. The air force has deployed its forces away from their home bases four times more often than during the Cold War. In 1996, the average soldier or marine was deployed more than 140 days. In 1986, the armed forces spent a total of 900,000 man-days on active missions. Seven years later, in 1993, that number was 6 million man-days, and in 1997, the U.S. military committed 13.2 million man-days to assigned missions. This exhausting pace was maintained by a force that was 36 percent smaller than it was at the height of the Cold War. Such overuse cannot continue.

REAL SOLUTIONS

Incredibly, some senior military leaders have responded to readiness problems by calling for *cuts* in training. The vice chairman of the Joint Chiefs of Staff has called for a reduction in the number of training exercises for army units, ships, and air wings so that those forces can be "more ready" for noncombat deployments and larger-scale exercises. But readiness means more than merely not using up supplies and parts. It also means training adequately and sufficiently so that our forces can accomplish their assigned missions with minimum casualties.

The long-term solution to today's readiness crisis does not lie in reducing required training. We need both to reduce the operations tempo of our forces and to restore the funding necessary to recruit and retain quality people. And that funding should not come at the expense of other military requirements. The chairman of the Joint Chiefs of Staff has estimated that today's extraordinarily high operations tempo has reached the point where to gain one dollar for readiness in any given year the military must give up five dollars of the modernization account used to replace worn-out equipment and to invest in new systems. That foregone modernization translates into increased readiness problems next year and the year after that. Such an approach simply mortgages our future readiness.

We must use the next several years to rebuild our forces, make critical long-term procurement decisions, and raise the morale of our armed forces. Only in this way can we prepare our forces for the changes in warfare and challenges that are likely to unfold over the next several decades.

It seems that every time we relax and start to believe conflict is a thing of the past, we get hit with a surprise. We were surprised and bloodied by the Japanese attack on Pearl Harbor in 1941. We were surprised again by the onset of the Korean conflict in 1950. We were surprised yet again in August 1990, when Saddam Hussein invaded Kuwait. Surprised—but this time prepared. Thanks to the Reagan military buildup of the 1980s, we were ready and able to send a half-million troops to the Persian Gulf. At the same time, we maintained a significant military presence in other parts of the world to deter aggression and defend our interests.

Early in 1999, the Clinton-Gore team recognized that America had begun to awaken to the sorry state of the country's military forces. The famed political instincts of this poll-driven crowd kicked in, and a few speeches on military preparedness were delivered. With great fanfare, the administration unveiled its first defense-budget increase. After dis-investing in defense for six years, the Clinton-Gore team is like the arsonist appearing before the city council and urging more fire trucks and higher pay for firefighters. Even the administration's own Joint Chiefs of Staff testified that the increase was far from what was required to address America's military needs.

I intend to put these issues front and center in the 2000 campaign, and I have no doubt that even Al Gore will adopt the rhetoric of a strong national defense. But the American people will look beyond the rhetoric and ask who is offering the better vision for our nation's future security. You will ask whom you can trust. I look forward to the debate.

21

Missile Defense

ASK YOURSELF what our military would do if a hostile country launched a missile at the territory of the United States. What would we do, for example, if North Korea were to launch a missile toward Alaska's Prudhoe Bay, where a significant percentage of the country's oil is produced, or if the People's Republic of China were to launch one of its Intercontinental Ballistic Missiles (ICBMs) at Los Angeles, as a Chinese general suggested could happen someday?

In fact, I have asked many Americans that question, and most of them respond that our military would simply shoot it down. They are often puzzled, then alarmed, then infuriated when I tell them the United States has *no* ability to shoot down ballistic missiles flying toward our country. As we prepare to enter a new century replete with new threats, our country must begin to consider soberly what we must do now, without delay, to protect ourselves.

There is no more serious issue facing this country than the threat of long-range missiles hitting the United States.

In 1997, Congress established a commission "to assess the nature and magnitude of the existing and emerging ballistic missile threat to the United States." Known as the Rumsfeld Commission after its chairman, the much-respected former defense secretary Donald Rumsfeld, the panel issued a stunning 1998 report with an eye-opening conclusion: Less than five years from now, a Third World nation could develop a ballistic missile capable of hitting the United States.

The Rumsfeld Commission concluded that a foreign missile threat could develop with little or no warning time. There were high-level dissenters to the Rumsfeld Report's conclusion. In August 1998, the chairman of the Joint Chiefs of Staff wrote to the U.S. Senate that the military had "different perspectives on likely time lines and associated warning times" for foreign missile developments than those put forth by the Rumsfeld Commission. The chairman stated that "we remain confident that the intelligence community can provide the necessary warning of indigenous development and deployment by a rogue state of an [ICBM] threat to the United States."

Sounds reassuring. Yet within days of the chairman's statement, North Korea fired the first of its Taepo Dong missiles, and U.S. intelligence agencies were surprised to learn that the Taepo Dong had a three-stage system capable of sending a warhead thirty-seven hundred miles away—enough range to reach Alaska or Hawaii.

Our intelligence agencies were also caught off guard by Iraq's invasion of Kuwait and later surprised to learn how advanced Saddam's chemical, biological, and nuclear operations were. Imagine our peril if these same agencies were to be surprised yet again by a hostile power's sudden announcement of ballistic missile capability and the threat to use it against American territory. In light of these realities, failure to deploy a missile defense is worse than irresponsible. The consequences of this failure could be catastrophic.

THREATS IN A NEW ENVIRONMENT

As of 1998, a total of thirty-six countries possessed ballistic missiles. Fourteen countries were producing or exporting these missiles. Six other countries were working on or had already acquired the capability to develop ballistic missiles on their own.

Though many of these nations claim that they are merely developing space-launch capability rather than militarily useful ballistic missiles, the fact is that there is little difference between a space-launch vehicle and a ballistic missile (other than payload and guidance system characteristics). Indeed, many of the space-launch vehicles in use today derive from ballistic missile technology. Conversely, space-launch vehicles can easily be modified into ballistic missiles armed with weapons of mass destruction.

As a result, not only do we face the existing missile forces and production capability of Russia and China but also the emerging forces of India, Pakistan, Iran, Iraq, and North Korea. The latter three states are not only proliferators. Each one places a high priority on being able to threaten U.S. territory, and each is working hard on developing the capability to do so. These nations believe that if they can threaten U.S. territory, the United States will not confront them in their own regions.

During the Cold War era, the Soviet Union tended to follow fairly predictable paths of development for new weapons, patterns that were observed and monitored by U.S. intelligence. The twenty-first century security environment promises to be very different. In a January 1999 speech at the Heritage Foundation in Washington, D.C., I indicated what my response to these new threats would be: "The next step is to develop a national missile defense system." I continued:

> Some will object that doing so would violate the ABM [Anti-Ballistic Missile] Treaty with the old Soviet Union. Let me offer a very simple question: Why should our ability to defend ourselves be short-circuited by a treaty signed in a completely different era—with a second party that is now literally nonexistent? It's a sign of how far we've fallen that more fidelity is shown to a piece of paper signed with a state that no longer exists than to our own Constitution. We should do now what we ought to have done long ago: declare the ABM Treaty obsolete and exercise our right to withdraw.

With the ABM Treaty set aside, my administration would deploy a ballistic missile defense system as soon as possible. I simply cannot fathom the thinking of those who are being penny-wise and pound-foolish about missile defense, who argue that such a deployment might cost around two billion dollars or more. We have already spent more than ten billion dollars in Bosnia. Deployment of a missile defense—which will inevitably be upgraded as technology advances—would be a sure sign to our adversaries that we intend to defend ourselves. It would be a sure sign that we do *not* intend to allow ourselves to be blackmailed into inaction by any regime that can get its hands on a ballistic missile with the range to reach the United States.

22

Terrorism

TERRORISTS do not play by the rules. What they understand is force, and I would use whatever force is necessary to protect Americans at home and abroad from the hatred and random violence of terrorists.

Sadly, it is now difficult to foresee a world without terrorism. Because modern media provide an instant audience for atrocity, fanatics know the world's cameras will flock to ruin and rubble, inadvertently helping the messengers of hate to communicate to the world in seconds.

The problem is frighteningly real. Terrorists blew up the Khobar Towers in Saudi Arabia in 1996, killing 19 U.S. Air Force personnel and injuring hundreds of others. Terrorists bombed the American embassies in Kenya and Tanzania last year, killing 200. The bombing of Pan Am flight 103 over Lockerbie, Scotland, took 270 lives, including those of 189 Americans.

The World Trade Center bombing erased any hope that America might be immune from terrorism on our home ground. Terrorists don't need complex missile systems to inflict casualties. A suitcase full of test tubes or a rental truck can serve as a "delivery system." The World Trade Center bombing left six dead and many injured. But how many Americans realize that the terrorists' actual plan was to release a cloud of sodium cyanide that had the potential to kill every person in the building?

You don't have to be an alarmist on these matters, only a realist. The world's only superpower is a natural target of every nut, every rogue dictator, every group with an ax to grind.

There are limited effective military responses to terrorism, and I certainly do not favor a wave of additional, Big Brother–type restrictions on civil liberties that would do little to effectively curb the threat. But we have to remind ourselves that leadership is about making choices. The real threat of terrorism has received nowhere near the attention it deserves.

Intelligence and global law enforcement cooperation are keys to dealing with the problem of terrorism. As Abraham Sofaer has pointed out, it is wrong to accept the Kenya and Tanzania bombings as an unavoidable consequence of terrorism; instead, we should regard the bombings as an intelligence failure. The monitoring of existing or suspected terrorist organizations must be a top priority for America's foreign-intelligence agencies, both through upgraded human intelligence—traditional infiltration of hostile groups—and electronic means. At the same time, the FBI and its counterparts in friendly nations need to improve their information-sharing efforts and their legal basis for joint action against terrorists.

When President Clinton ordered the cruise missile attack on terrorists in Afghanistan, public scrutiny focused on his motive: Did he launch the attack to divert attention from his day of grand jury testimony, his admission of deceit, and his disastrous and petulant attack on the independent counsel earlier in the week? Those were the wrong questions. The first question should have been, Why was there no warning of the attacks on the embassies in Africa?

The second question should have been, Why had there been no preemptive attacks on the terrorists, given their record of threats against the United States? It's clear that the Clinton-Gore administration was aware of terrorist Osama bin Laden's culpability in prior attacks on U.S. facilities, his commitment to continuing those attacks, and his pursuit of training and planning operations in Afghanistan. In fact, just weeks before the bombings, bin Laden was indicted (in a sealed indictment) by the U.S. Department of Justice for soliciting the murder of Americans.

The third question should have been, Why just a gesture? Why not the sort of assault in strength that would have assured the destruction of bin Laden's organization and perhaps the capture of intelligence necessary to shut its doors for a decade?

Terrorism cannot be combated by half-measures delivered too late and with no substantial follow-up. The Clinton-Gore administration's reflexive rejection of force until a crisis arrives and force is compelled is exactly the wrong approach.

23

Israel and the Peace Process

FOR THREE DECADES, U.S. policy has been to assist efforts to find peace in the Middle East between Israel and the Arab states and peoples. Our goal has been to create a community of interests among moderate Arab states and Israel, leading to greater regional peace and stability for both. With U.S. help, much has been accomplished. Israel is now formally at peace with two of its neighbors, Egypt and Jordan, and it is actively engaged in a "peace process" with the Palestinian Liberation Organization.

However, the leaders who brought the region through many wars and to the brink of a comprehensive peace are passing from the scene. The death of King Hussein of Jordan in February 1999 was the latest of these losses.

It is essential that we anchor our Middle East policy around a core strategic fact: Democratic Israel is and must remain our closest ally in the region. American statecraft should never forget that fact or, worse, take it for granted.

However, that is precisely what has happened under the Clinton-Gore administration. Through its handling of the peace process, the administration has transformed the once "special relationship" between the United States and Israel into one in which Israel's outstanding security concerns are made secondary to keeping the PLO leadership satisfied. As Elliott Abrams has noted, "They now treat Arafat—who the day before yesterday was ordering the murder of Americans—far more respectfully than they do the prime minister of Israel."

The process itself is based on the following quid pro quo: The PLO promised to end its armed struggle against Israel's existence and implement a series of security measures designed to end Palestinian violence and terrorism aimed at Israel. In return, the PLO received recognition, grants of territory in the Israeli-occupied West Bank, and the right to rule over that territory. By any objective measure, Israel has kept its side of the bargain while the PLO has failed to carry out its end of the Oslo and Wye Plantation agreements. In a tragic and ironic footnote to the peace process, more Israelis have died in the four years since Oslo than during the six previous years, and the PLO leadership still encourages Palestinians to think of Israelis as the enemy.

The key problem is that the Clinton administration has placed too much emphasis on the need to keep the peace process going, as though the process were an end in itself. In practice, this has produced a policy of minimizing the PLO's failure to carry out its pledges, maximizing pressure on Israel to continue making concessions, and adopting an American stance of professed "neutrality" between our democratic ally and the nondemocratic PLO.

So what should be done? First, the United States should focus its efforts on the straightforward proposition that both sides should comply with their previous commitments made at Oslo and at the Wye Plantation. Second, the United States should not allow its effort to help the peace process along to obscure its relationship with Israel. We may, and should be, an honest broker for peace, but we are not neutral between the two parties. We are interested in the peace process only to the extent that it results in a situation in which Israel finds itself more secure, not less, at the end of the day. Accomplishing that objective obviously carries with it the promise that Israel's neighbors will likewise find their interests served.

Third, we should not ignore the lessons of the past when it comes to negotiating peace and arms-control accords. It's not the agreement that ultimately counts but the character of the governments who have signed it and must carry out its terms. Palestinians are now ruled by an autocratic and corrupt leadership with a tendency toward violence. This should make us wary of forcing an agreement on Israel unless it is fully satisfied with its terms, and it should lead us to reject calls for a Palestinian state until its rulers can be trusted to govern in a manner that leads to peace instead of continuing confrontation.

24

Russia:
Opportunity Imperiled

PRESIDENT George Bush left his successor a superb foreign policy position in Central and Eastern Europe. The Soviet Union had crumbled. German unity was assured. Russia stood in the springtime of freedom with the prospect of true democracy and real economic reform ahead of it.

But the Clinton-Gore team blew it. They preferred diplomatic form rather than substance, photo-ops rather than thoughtful policies, and pleasant press conferences instead of meaningful dialogue. So the most significant Russian revolution, the one that occurred in 1991 rather than the one in 1917, now teeters on the verge of failure.

President Boris Yeltsin is chronically ill. The Communist Party dominates Russia's national legislature. To make matters worse, Russia is literally bankrupt, having defaulted on its international obligations, and its internal economy is in chaos.

Poorly framed Western (and largely American) economic advice, combined with Russian officialdom's willingness to bilk both the International Monetary Fund and the Russian people, has resulted in a devastating economic contraction. The vast majority of Russians are suffering while a tiny elite has profited handsomely by milking the state during the transition from communism. The resulting collapse of production has brought the country's GNP down to less than half its 1990 levels. Approximately fifty million Russians live below a poverty line that is already ridiculously low.

One political result is that anti-Western and anti-American nationalism is on the rise. The pro-Western economic reformers have been discredited and are out of power. The IMF money and the Western financial aid totaling over seventy billion dollars since 1992 appears largely to have been wasted. It's even possible that part of it was recycled out of Russia and into Swiss and Cypriot bank accounts by corrupt officials and businessmen tied directly to criminal syndicates.

Russia is not truly a democracy. It has an authoritarian presidential system in which the leader is selected by popular vote but can rule by decree in most matters. Because power remains so heavily concentrated in the president (and his representative, the prime minister), Russia remains politically unstable. It remains a government of men rather than one of institutions regulated by law. While the prime minister exercises significant authority, his power derives from the presidency rather than from either parliament (the Duma) or the people. The absence of a cooperative relationship between the presidency and the Duma reflects the underdeveloped nature of law as the basis of government in a country with almost no legislative tradition.

In reality, today's Russia is ruled by an oligarchy of competing patronage circles. The political and economic competition to determine key government decisions takes place outside the view of the public. No wonder that patronage, corruption, and private violence are more important than idealism, civic virtue, or ideology in the motives of politicians and their business counterparts.

In Russia today, the *nomenklatura*, the "new class" that arose under communism, has become the aristocracy of the post-communist era. Having controlled the game under the Bolsheviks, high party officials and factory managers took unfair advantage of the privatization process to monopolize wealth and power. As a result, the power and privilege of the Soviet upper class were transformed into the property interests of the new Russia with little or no opportunities for ordinary citizens to join the elite.

If Russia did not have thirty thousand nuclear warheads and a capacity to launch them, U.S. policy could safely ignore Russia's travails in the short run. But Russia's rising nationalism in everything from the sale of dangerous technologies abroad to the country's unwillingness to play a responsible role in Iraq represents an ominous trend. A new policy model for dealing with Russia is urgently needed. That model should be part economic, part political, and part social.

To fashion the first part, we have to recognize that there isn't really a single Russian economy but three that function simultaneously. One is the "virtual economy" of the old state enterprises and former collective farms. Another is what Russians call wild capitalism, through which the new Russian elite extract wealth and send it abroad in concert with organized crime, corrupt government officials, phony banks, and controlled media. The third is real capitalism, in which industrious individuals run small businesses. This is by far the smallest and most vulnerable sector, but it is also the most promising.

America's policy should be to ensure that outside assistance to Russia supports the men and women engaged in real free enterprise. This means selectively providing help on a project-by-project basis to the localities where the legal and financial framework for economic freedom is being created. The corrupt forces in Moscow must understand that assistance will be available only on one condition: that it be internationally administered directly to areas and projects where it would be helpful.

That assistance should emphasize the production and distribution of food in Russia. Hunger should be an anomaly in a land so rich and among a people so hardworking. The United States should take the lead among the world's wealthy nations to share our technology and enterprise to restore Russia's agricultural base. Unless the food situation improves there, the prospects for violence and instability will increase.

One key to Russia's long-range recovery is the extraction of its rich natural resources. The industries involved in that enterprise are both the critical problem and the major hope for rescuing the Russian economy. These tremendous assets are actually declining in value as a result of corruption, mismanagement, and a glut on international markets. America should encourage Western corporations to purchase controlling interests and reform these companies so they conform to accepted international business practices. Whether the Russians choose to accept investments under terms of good governance will be up to them.

On the political front, we must deal more realistically with whatever leaders control Moscow and the central bureaucratic, military, and political organizations. On this level, programs for cataloging and dismantling nuclear weapons can be expanded. While we have spent nearly three billion dollars since 1992 to dismantle Russian missiles and build storage facilities for nuclear materials, we have authorized less than a hundred million dollars over the next five years to assist in the dismantling of the warheads themselves. That is a misplaced priority.

The next administration must accept the possibility of continuing instability in Russia and be careful to keep the lines of communication open to all sides there. We can assume that whichever group controls the Russian presidency will probably represent the corrupt elements of Russia's virtual economy and wild capitalism rather than the interests of the Russian people. It is therefore essential that U.S. policy should not become hostage to any faction there. Although we must, at times, deal with unsavory personalities, we should maintain equal distance from all those competing for power.

The third part of our new model may be both the most important and the most difficult. It is nothing less than the creation of a value system that can sustain Russia's experiment in democracy. To foster respect for law—and laws worth respecting—we should provide small grants for legal education, encourage private funding for pilot enterprises in key economic sectors, and assist the formation of modern, reform-minded political parties. Only when the corrupt values of the Soviet era are as dead as Lenin himself will freedom and prosperity be secure in the new Russia.

Foreigners cannot transform Russian society and culture, but we can help those Russians who are trying to do so. Let's put their current situation into historical context. This is a people who have suffered hellishly through most of the twentieth century. They have been enslaved by their own rulers, butchered by Nazis, and betrayed at every turn by their own political leaders. Yet they have endured.

The Russian people are the heirs of an ancient civilization and an enduring faith. Like Ronald Reagan, I will go to Russia, not just to confer with its leaders, but to address the Russian people. I will bring to them, from the heart of America, this assurance: Through their years of sadness, the Russian people were never our enemy. In these days of their hardship, we should be their best friends in the world. Just as we rejoiced in their liberation, so now we stand ready to help them achieve their rightful place in the family of freedom.

25

A Conflict with China?

MY INTEREST in China is keen and personal. My eldest son lives there and is fluent in Mandarin Chinese. I have visited China three times since leaving office. I want China to succeed. I want someday to welcome China into the family of democratic nations. I want to see China's growth rate and per capita income reach much higher levels.

In short, I don't perceive China as our enemy. But neither is it a "strategic partner," as the Clinton administration puts it. A partnership implies common values and similar goals. Neither are present today, though we should work to develop them.

On my trips to the People's Republic of China, I have enjoyed extensive conversations with President Jiang Zemin, Foreign Minister Qian Qichen, former vice premier and now Premier Zhu Rongji, and Hong Kong Chief Executive Teng Cee-hwa. I have taken the measure of the PRC leadership. They are a determined and confident group of nationalists, and a few remain committed Leninists.

We need to recognize the emergence of a "new China." China is much different than it was ten or even five years ago. The new China is increasingly assertive and aggressive in the wake of some profound changes around the world.

On one trip, in 1993, I was extensively lectured by the vice chair of the Chinese army's general staff in a revealing and most alarming fashion on China's military prowess. Five years later, when Congressman Christopher Cox reported on the People's Liberation Army's insatiable search for technology, I was not surprised. The PRC is even now modernizing its army and beginning to build a blue-water navy that is reminiscent of the naval buildup of Imperial Germany at the beginning of this century, when that country sought to force its way into prominence as a world power.

One of the books I assigned to students in the graduate school course I've been teaching is *The Coming Conflict with China* by Richard Bernstein and Ross Munro. I don't agree with all of the authors' conclusions, but they do make many astute observations. They argue that when the Soviet Union dissolved, Chinese leaders concluded that the collapse occurred because political freedom outstripped economic development. And they vowed not to let the same thing happen in China. China watched as Iraq, supposedly a major regional power with a formidable military machine, was defeated in one of the most lopsided wars of all time. If acquiring American-style technological superiority wasn't a priority for China before the Gulf War, it surely was afterward.

And increasingly, high-level Chinese officials apply to us the rhetoric once reserved for the Soviet Union—words like "hegemonist," which carry a clear-cut message: America is now the threat. And the message is directed principally at our treaty alliances with countries like Japan and South Korea as well as our strategic and economic partnerships with many others in the Pacific. The irony is that the term "hegemonist" more aptly applies to China itself.

As much as we need to focus on the conduct and actions of the People's Republic of China, it is long past time for us to focus on our own conduct. When President Clinton visited China in 1998, he allowed his Chinese hosts to demand that he participate in a state ceremony in Tiananmen Square. I visited forty-seven countries as vice president, and I know that host countries will make a variety of requests. But the president has ultimate control over his own schedule. Going to Tiananmen Square was a mistake; it sent a terrible message.

Moreover, on Chinese soil, President Clinton criticized and snubbed key American allies such as Japan. On Chinese soil, he not only humiliated Taiwan, he went further and slyly changed American policy toward Taiwan. These were profoundly harmful acts. And we need to call this what it is—a policy of appeasement.

As we assess what our policy toward China should be, the first thing to do is to confront some truths. Most of us in the Bush administration, certainly President Bush and I, believed that a policy that encouraged trade, with a minimum of sanctions and sanctimony, would more likely move China toward greater freedom for its people and a more productive relationship between our two countries. We were firm when we had to be, particularly in the wake of the horrendous massacre at Tiananmen Square.

We pursued worthy objectives. But upon reflection, it is clear to me that the Chinese took advantage of that opportunity. The next truth is that the situation is far worse today. In six years of one administration, we have witnessed the following in China:

- A continued decline in human rights;
- An increase in religious persecution, particularly of the house church movement;

- Interference in our national elections;
- An increase in China's role in the proliferation of weapons of mass destruction;
- Threats against Taiwan and aggressive moves against the Philippines in the South China Sea;
- Not-so-veiled threats against America;
- Espionage involving our most critical secrets; and
- Repeated controversies surrounding China's acquisition of high technology designed to deliver weapons of mass destruction.

That's quite a list. The question now is, How we can improve the situation? The most frequently suggested course is to penalize China by removing the Most Favored Nation status we bestow on it—now known as normal trade relations—and delaying China's entry into the World Trade Organization.

At a minimum, we should insist that trade with China be conducted on a level playing field. Until China commits itself to that level playing field, it is absurd to give up the huge leverage of the annual Most Favored Nation decision, as the Clinton administration has done for all practical purposes.

But more important is the moral issue. President Clinton has consistently supported granting China Most Favored Nation status no matter how egregious the human rights abuses documented by his own State Department and no matter how many documented cases there are of China assisting in the spread of weapons of mass destruction. But when Chinese companies were producing pirated American films, CDs, and music recordings, the United States government swung into action, threatening to impose tariff increases of 100 percent if such copyright violations continued. The Chinese government responded by taking at least some steps to correct the problem, although the results were weak.

Doesn't it strike you as a little odd that our government is willing to go to these lengths for music but not for human rights? It is time we stop thinking of the Chinese simply as one billion customers and start thinking of them as one billion human beings.

China wants to be part of the World Trade Organization, and I believe it is clearly in our interest—and the world's—to have China participate in a body that can mediate trade disputes. So the question is *when*, not *if*. But there is no reason to rush this decision. The Chinese have to make significant changes. Until that happens, too many unanswered questions remain to resolve the WTO question for China.

Taiwan, on the other hand, clearly meets the criteria for admission into the WTO. We should support Taiwan's immediate entry into the WTO without letting the People's Republic of China set any preconditions. After all, Taiwan is our seventh largest trading partner, with a free market that makes it the world's twentieth largest economy.

The failure of the Clinton-Gore China policies is rooted in a failure of will and leadership. It is difficult to say what the single worst moment was in the last six years of our China policy, but among the worst has to be when President Clinton went to China and tilted our policy against democratic Taiwan. In a chilling statement, he pronounced the "three no's" desired by the PRC: "We don't support independence for Taiwan, or two Chinas, or one Taiwan and one China. And we don't believe that Taiwan should be a member in any organization for which statehood is a requirement." The administration claims this represented no change in policy. In fact, President Clinton is the first American president ever to publicly articulate the three no's. This was a great victory for China because it formalized Taiwan's diplomatic isolation.

There is a long-term danger here. In my view, President Jimmy Carter made a critical error in the late seventies by breaking diplomatic relations with Taiwan. But we in Congress tried to undo some of the damage by passing the Taiwan Relations Act to ensure that we helped Taiwan meet its defense needs. Since passage of the Taiwan Relations Act in 1979, every administration has ensured that the PRC understands the importance of peacefully resolving issues relating to Taiwan. I communicated exactly this message to Chinese leaders myself on several occasions. Yet the message is not getting through anymore. In 1995, a Chinese general questioned whether we would be willing to trade "Los Angeles for Taipei." In 1996, just prior to free elections in Taiwan, the PRC conducted extensive live-fire exercises off Taiwan. No one even pretended that this was not an exercise in intimidation. And to his credit, President Clinton did send two aircraft carrier battle groups to the area.

This, then, is the context in which President Clinton made his unfortunate statements about Taiwan. What if the growing independence movement in Taiwan succeeds in taking power? According to President Clinton, we don't support independence. So if Taiwan were to declare independence and the PRC attacked Taiwan, what would we do? And, most importantly, after watching the United States pander to the PRC on the Taiwan issue, would a member of the Chinese central committee conclude that America is willing to stand firm in defense of Taiwan? The fact that this is a legitimate question is very troubling—and very dangerous.

Diplomacy takes many forms and is often best done in private. But there are times when clear public statements are imperative. If I am elected president I will deliver a message to the Chinese leadership that makes clear that the resolution of these issues will be handled peacefully. China must not even consider attacking Taiwan.

But we should also take some concrete steps now. We should move forward on providing Taiwan and key allies like Japan and South Korea the ability to protect themselves through theater missile defenses.

A Conflict with China?

As I said at the outset of this chapter, I want to see a free and prosperous China. Has that goal been advanced in the last six years? I don't think so. What have we accomplished? According to President Clinton's breathless announcement, China and the United States have stopped targeting each other with nuclear missiles. But missiles can be retargeted in a matter of minutes. The world is a little more dangerous today because of the policies that underlie fatuous statements like those made by an American president.

The best way to approach China is from a position of strength, at the head of a coalition of democratic nations with open economies: Japan, Korea, Australia, the Philippines, Thailand, and, in the future, perhaps even India and Indonesia. To approach China alone and directly is to place the United States in the position of being a supplicant to the Middle Kingdom. This is exactly the trap into which President Clinton fell during his China trip. To approach China as a friend who nonetheless leads a coalition of Asian democracies is to place China in a position in which it must either behave responsibly or alienate most of the outside world that matters to its future.

We should make clear to the People's Republic of China that we will not barter away the cause of human liberty and security among nations in exchange for increased sales. We should make clear that respect is a two-way street. We should make clear that the first step toward a productive relationship is honesty. We should make clear that we want nothing more than to have China enter the full community of nations—whatever the venue—but that everyone else has to play by the rules, and China would have to as well.

What I have outlined here may be seen as a tough policy. But I firmly believe that our goal of peace and prosperity in the Pacific will be met only through firmness and respect.

26

Kyoto or Kuwait

AMERICA ought to lead the world, not be led by it. The United States should direct; it should not be driven. Either we have confidence in our system of laws and assert the superiority of our core ideals, or we allow ourselves to become just one system among many, one country with rights and interests no greater or less than any other country in the world.

People who think our country is uniquely good and uniquely blessed are called "American exceptionalists." I am an exceptionalist, unafraid to declare that America is the greatest country in the history of the world. It is more virtuous, more generous, stronger, and wiser than any other power in history.

It is our unique institutions that allow America to claim leadership in the community of nations. Twice we have provided the difference between the subjugation of Europe and its liberation, first from Hitler and then during the Cold War. From 1945 until the fall of the Soviet Union, the United States protected that portion of the world that had not already fallen under communist domination. We set the stage for the liberation of oppressed peoples around the globe. Time and time again—in Korea, Vietnam, the Middle East, Grenada, Panama, Nicaragua, and ultimately the Gulf War—the United States stood against aggression and tyranny and for peace and freedom.

America's claim to world leadership rests on its values. We lead not because of our firepower but because of our commitment to freedom. Because our country remains the world's greatest hope for peaceful progress, we must defend the values that America embodies. We must remain that "city on a hill." Our leadership role is, however, threatened by two forces.

First, around the globe other countries question whether American values have changed and whether those new values are worth importing. It is not only American conservatives who see the abandonment of middle-class values as a cause of great concern. If a country's leaders do not respect their oaths of office, can that country be expected to honor its international commitments?

Second, the feckless approach to foreign policy practiced by the Clinton administration has established a record of unreliability and incoherence.

Contrast our response to Saddam's invasion of Kuwait with Al Gore's abdication to the international bureaucrats meeting in Kyoto.

When Saddam invaded Kuwait, President Bush quickly declared, "This will not stand." Then we set about assembling and leading a coalition with the clearly articulated purpose of driving Saddam out of Kuwait. Our success depended on keeping our word.

Secretary of Defense Dick Cheney and Gen. Colin Powell were immediately dispatched to Saudi Arabia. I was dispatched to hostile territory: the Congress. From the first day of the crisis, we engaged the support of the international community. But our moves were not dictated by, only coordinated with, the UN. Had we not led, Saddam would today still occupy Kuwait City and perhaps the whole of the Arabian peninsula as well. When I spent New Year's Eve and New Year's Day with our troops in the Saudi desert and aboard the aircraft carrier USS *John F. Kennedy,* I spoke with them about the mission of America, not the UN, as leader of the free world.

Contrast that record of stressing American leadership with the record of the Clinton-Gore administration embracing the UN-led efforts to push for American deindustrialization in the Kyoto accord. In Kyoto, foreign bureaucrats demanded American acquiescence to emission standards that would, if ever implemented, be a disaster for American agriculture and cripple American competitiveness—while doing nothing to reduce the global volume of so-called "greenhouse gases."

This treaty represents a systematic and concerted push to surrender important aspects of American sovereignty to international organizations—for no purpose. What powers would the United States relinquish to a global climate-control authority? Suppose such an entity found America in violation. Could it shut down entire industries? Require plant closings? Dictate American forestry policy? No one knows for sure.

What we do know is that the administration is devoted to the Kyoto treaty, though fortunately the agreement has no chance of being ratified by the Senate. The Clinton-Gore administration intends to get around this problem by implementing the treaty's requirements through executive action. This is unacceptable arrogance, and it flies in the face of the Constitution.

The stark contrast between my approach and Al Gore's was also evident in his statement following the deaths of fifteen Americans in a "friendly fire" incident in the no-fly zone over Iraq in 1994. "I want to extend condolences," Gore said, "to the families of those who died in the service of the United Nations." This was not a misstatement. Al Gore believes the UN ought to lead the world.

The Somalia mission, begun by President Bush as a humanitarian relief effort, was distorted under President Clinton into the fuzzy "nation-building" that UN Secretary General Boutros Boutros-Ghali had originally urged on me in a meeting in December 1992. I rejected his demand on behalf of our administration because we recognized it as an invitation to a quagmire. The United States had no business adopting the hopeless, UN-directed task of nation-building in a land where no sense of nationhood even existed. But it didn't take long for the UN leadership to turn the Clinton-Gore team into "nation-builders" in an incompetent set of moves for which American troops paid with their lives. That is the most tangible cost of the sacrifice of our sovereignty.

As the world becomes more economically integrated, we need to be vigilant in preserving our sovereignty. America's control over its own destiny must never be subject to the veto of global bureaucrats or ideological opponents of our leadership. As Cornell University professor Jeremy Rabkin explains in his recent book *Why Sovereignty Matters:* "Sovereignty denotes independence. A sovereign state is one that acknowledges no superior power over its own government—or, as the Declaration of Independence put it, with proper piety, no superior 'among the powers of the Earth.'"

Sovereignty is about accountability. We, the people, make the laws through our elected representatives. Every time we pledge to take direction from international organizations rather than our own institutions, we limit our right of self-government.

The United Nations must not be given powers to control United States policy, regardless of how high-minded the goals. American military action should not be dictated by the United

Nations, and U.S. soldiers should never be placed under foreign command. And no American policy or personnel should be placed under jurisdiction of the UN's proposed "International Criminal Court."

Beyond that, it's certainly not too much to ask that UN officials stay out of local politics in America. Look at what happened in the American West just a few years ago. In 1995, the Clinton-Gore administration invited a team of inspectors from the UN's World Heritage Committee to evaluate a proposed mining venture on the fringe of Yellowstone National Park. Naturally, area residents were infuriated by the notion that international inspectors should have any input whatsoever on a local land-use question. But since Yellowstone Park had been designated a "world heritage site" by the UN, environmental activists took the initiative to invite the UN, and the administration gladly obliged.

The entire episode appeared ludicrous to almost everybody, especially since the World Heritage Committee operates under the auspices of UNESCO, a UN agency from which the United States withdrew many years ago. But it was no joke to the environmental activists who wanted to manipulate the American political process or to the compliant Clinton-Gore administration. No American leader should allow such a usurpation of our sovereignty.

Sovereignty concerns arise outside the UN as well. The North American Free Trade Agreement, while representing a positive step forward for America's economy, was saddled by the Clinton-Gore administration with side agreements that basically committed the United States to maintaining certain environmental and labor laws on our books. Such commitments tie the hands of future Congresses and violate the principle of representative government. We should not go down that road again.

There can be no more obvious difference in leadership than the difference represented by the examples of Kyoto and Kuwait. In Kyoto, America surrendered its leadership and part of its sovereignty. In Kuwait, America led and restored the sovereignty of a conquered country.

Kyoto or Kuwait: It's a stark choice, and one I trust the American people to make.

PART 6

A Future Worth Fighting For

A good politician with nerve and a program that is right can win in the face of the stiffest opposition.

—HARRY S. TRUMAN

27

A Future Worth Fighting For

Dᴜʀɪɴɢ ᴍʏ dozen years in the Congress, I met with thousands of visitors. The folks from Indiana often remarked how inspiring it was to visit the Capitol—the "seat of power," they would often call it.

If you have been to the Capitol, you know what they meant. To walk through either wing, under the Rotunda, or onto the floor of either the House or the Senate is to feel a part of the American epic. Every corner of the building is full of history.

Sometimes when I had a free hour or two, I'd go out for a run on the Mall. Usually I'd loop down and around the Washington Monument. On good days, I'd make it to the Lincoln Memorial and back. I'm convinced it's the best running path in the world.

On every one of these runs, I would always look with pride on the Capitol as I completed the course. It is the symbol of the country, the building wherein the people's representatives are supposed to be doing the people's business. And within that building, too, is ultimately contained the power of this amazing nation. The view of the Capitol from the Mall never fails to inspire, because it's so much more than a building. It's an idea laid out in stone.

The idea of doing the people's business has fallen on hard times. Items of the people's business that have gone undone include the term-limits legislation that has not been passed, the tax cuts that go undelivered, the strong national defense that has eroded these past six years.

At a right angle to the Mall are the grounds of the White House. Every president who has ever lived there has been obliged by the Constitution to swear that he will "faithfully execute the office of the president of the United States, and will to the best of my ability, preserve, protect, and defend the Constitution of the United States." In recent years, that oath has been breached. As a result, many Americans now doubt whether anyone in public life is bound by his word.

I am. And I will be. And I will set about doing the real business of the American people. My campaign for the presidency will lay out what I think that business should be.

Ideas win elections, but only when they are the centerpiece of a campaign. Republicans lost the presidency in 1992 and 1996—and barely held Congress in 1998—because their campaigns were dominated by personality rather than issues. Republicans won in 1980, 1984, 1988, and 1994 because their campaigns were organized and inspired by bold visions of what America could be. Ronald Reagan understood the need to communicate ideas to the electorate. So did the Republican congressional leadership in 1994 when it proposed the Contract with America.

Winning campaigns lay an agenda before the American people and never lose sight of it. If the agenda being debated on election eve is your opponent's, you have already lost. If, on the other hand, it is *your* agenda that defines the campaign, even should it be hotly debated, you will win.

To push ideas forward requires both adherence to bedrock principles and the courage of one's convictions. A campaign is doomed if it is dominated in the areas of policy, strategy, and tactics by swivel-chair experts within the Washington Beltway who try to follow public opinion rather than shape it.

I believe strongly in the famed Eleventh Commandment, which says, "Speak no ill of a fellow Republican." I have never attacked a fellow Republican, and I certainly will not start now. But I am going to defend Republicans against the slanders that they lack compassion. And I am going to defend the courageous House managers who led the impeachment of Bill Clinton. I am going to fight for the middle class, and I intend to voice the concerns of all Americans regardless of class, color, or age. I intend to especially champion the family. It remains the building block of everything good in our nation.

Conservatives have always been compassionate. They understood long before the elites figured it out that the Great Society, however well intentioned, was destroying poor families. They understood long ago that racial quotas could never bring America together but would only divide it and deepen animosity. And they have always understood that genuine compassion means leaving hardworking Americans with more of their money with which to provide for their families and support their churches and charities.

I am going to redefine the Republican Party. We are not the party of big business interests, nor are we the party of Barbra Streisand, Jane Fonda, Ted Turner, or other big wallets with big voices but little faith in the American people. Rather, the Republican Party is built on the values of middle America and the hopes of all those who aspire to climb the opportunity ladder. It knows the problems of both waitress moms and soccer moms. It knows the fears that parents have for the safety of their children in today's violent culture. And it understands why so many Americans are alienated from the government and feel that government does not care about them.

Sometimes conservatives may be tempted to abandon politics, so deep is their alienation. Sometimes the debasement of the country's culture seems so pronounced that they cannot see any benefit in continuing the fight.

That's wrong. Just ask any parent who is rearing children. We cannot abandon the struggle for a good, kind, caring, decent, and secure America, because we cannot abandon America's children. More than anything else, it's the kids who are worth fighting for.

Those who are discouraged should keep in mind the example of William Wilberforce. This long-serving member of the British Parliament took up the cause of abolishing the slave trade within the British Empire in 1788 when he offered to Parliament a twelve-point proposal to do just that. He never abandoned the cause. Wilberforce finally succeeded in 1807, having overcome the opposition of some of the wealthiest and most influential Englishmen of his day.

The difficulty of the challenge is usually proportionate to the reward. And where the future of our country is concerned, the rewards will be great indeed.

We don't need rhetorical compassion for the young. We need a deep and unyielding commitment to renewing American ideals and restoring American culture to the values that propelled it to victory in World War II and that launched its postwar prosperity in the fifties and early sixties. The twin goals of the next presidency must be returning America to the best traditions of its past while allowing all its entrepreneurial spirit and energy to make the future far greater than we could even imagine.

To move America in this direction will require a long and sustained fight; it will involve political conflict, and it will not be easy. The culture has changed dramatically because a relatively few people saw that there was money to be made and power to be gained by taking it over. Taking back our culture from the privileged elites who now dominate it will require sacrifice and long commitment, and there will be setbacks along the way. But we cannot give up either our principles or the effort.

That effort depends upon four cornerstones, four "faiths": faith in God, faith in freedom, faith in our families, and faith in the next generation. As a God-fearing and freedom-loving people, we must discipline ourselves and not rely on the government to do so. We must always choose the policies and practices that increase the freedom of individuals and families to do what they want and become what they dream. And we must trust that the next generation will prove their critics wrong and gladly assume the burdens of political leadership.

If we want to leave our country as well off, strong, and principled as the one left us by the World War II generation, the choices I have detailed in this book must be made, and they must be made soon. I hope you make those choices with me. In return, I want to make you ten promises—promises worth fighting for.

First, I will stand firm for the values that are the foundation of America's greatness, and I will appoint judges who will respect those values, not undermine them by substituting their own views for the wisdom of the people.

Second, I will defend the value of human life. And I will push Congress to immediately send me legislation ending partial-birth abortion.

Third, I will cut income tax rates by 30 percent across the board. It is time to unleash the full potential of our economy, provide more opportunity for every American, and lighten the burden on working families.

Fourth, I will put Freedom Accounts into place to help the middle class save for the critical needs of life—healthcare, college education, the long-term care of our parents, and our own retirement security.

Fifth, I will push political reform by championing term limits and by taking an ax to the federal government. The bureaucracy is out of control, and its growth threatens our heritage of freedom. With a Republican Congress, we will be able to finally take on and downsize the government, and we must begin with the most feared and most powerful federal bureaucracy, the IRS.

Sixth, I will protect our senior citizens who receive social security and Medicare from any decline in their benefits. We must reform both systems and provide the next generation with more choices to better plan for their retirement, but reform must never come at the expense of those who built this country's present prosperity.

Seventh, every policy my administration undertakes will be subject to two tests: (1) Is this a proper function of the federal government? and (2) Does it strengthen the American family? As I've repeated all across our country, we cannot have a great nation without healthy and strong families. That means parents and children must have the freedom to create stable and protected environments in which children can grow to maturity.

Eighth, I will insist that Congress pass legislation returning authority and federal education dollars to those most important to our children's education: parents, school districts, and the states.

Ninth, I will build and begin to deploy a ballistic missile defense. Nothing is more important than the physical safety of our people. It should have been done by now, but I will certainly get it done.

Tenth, I promise you that the era of compromise and shortcuts on matters of integrity, honor, and accountability will be over the day I take office. Character does count, and leaders can live up to the standards we set for our families. The long national soap opera will end in January 2001.

These are ten promises worth fighting for, and I will pursue them with zeal and with the good humor that ought always to mark our national debates.

Today's politics is deeply diseased—there's no denying that. The Clinton-Gore campaign of 1992 ushered in an era of permanent attack politics that has left us awash in cynicism and dispirited at the decline of civility in our public life.

I hope to change that. Marilyn and I have loved every minute of our public life, both in and out of elected office. We are old-fashioned patriots, and we have never been able to understand those who fail to see the full glory of this country and to recognize God's unique blessings upon it. We are both aware of how the dreams of many are still far from fulfillment and that some of our nation's problems are truly daunting.

But none of these challenges, none of these problems, will defeat the hard work and good will of the American people.

The new century can be another great American century, but only if we rededicate ourselves to the purposes and principles that served us so well during two world wars and the Cold War.

When the nation is led by men and women who believe in the people's goodness and in God's grace, there is nothing we cannot accomplish.

The decision to renew America is ultimately not the president's. It is the people's. Lincoln, in his first inaugural address, made this point. The union would be dissolved only if the people chose to do so, and it would be preserved only if the people chose to save it. That is still true. With all my heart, I believe they will make the right choice. And together, we will make our country new again.

After all, America is worth fighting for.

Acknowledgments

Many wonderful and talented people have helped me prepare for this campaign and write this book. The organization of my proposals and the development of detailed plans has taken many years, and the effort has been very focused over the past few months.

As with my first two books, my principal editor and closest collaborator has been Marilyn. We have always been and will always remain a team.

Hugh Hewitt, John McConnell, and Kyle McSlarrow have spent months with me and my notes. Kyle is my talented campaign manager and a closet policy wonk who is involved with the nuts and bolts of elections because they are the keys to the implementation of ideas. John is the necessary ingredient to anyone serving in high public office—a talented and loyal aide of absolute integrity. Hugh brought a California perspective and Ohio common sense to the project, both of which are necessary to any book on America. I could not have completed the manuscript without all three of them.

Hugh's assistant, Lynne Chapman, kept track of the manuscript and an avalanche of edits. I thank her as well.

Tom Duesterberg, my top aide in the Senate and a dependable friend whose counsel I have valued for many years, made extremely useful contributions throughout the endeavor. Keith Rabois is a tireless researcher with an eagle eye who read each draft and made helpful comments on every page. He has now become a member of my staff. Dan Troy and my spokesman, Jonathan Baron, offered many astute and timely suggestions. I'm most grateful to them all.

As always, Bill Gribbin, my longtime confidant and a true political and historical savant, gave lots of advice, all of it good.

My friend and wonderful editor, Midge Decter, with her discernment and intellect, helped me refine the text.

I've also benefited greatly from the keen suggestions of close friends Karl Jackson, Gov. John Sununu, Chuck Colson, Jack Vardaman, Sen. Dan Coats, Rep. David McIntosh, Jeff Bergner, Jack Kemp, and Les Lenkowsky.

Special contributions were made by Andrew Peyton Thomas, Jeffrey McKitrick, Dave Juday, Bruce Herschensohn, Peter Rusthoven, Gail Wilensky, Herb London, Gary Schmitt, Mark Lagon, John Cohrssen, and Gary Geipel.

I'm also grateful for input received from Michael Joyce, Bill Bennett, Gov. Carroll Campbell, John Hillen, Donald Rumsfeld, Mark Albrecht, Sen. Spence Abraham, Joseph Shattan, Michael Novak, Lawrence Kudlow, Stephen Moore, Cesar Conda, Henry Sokolski, Jude Wanniski, Peter Signorelli, Barbara McLennan, Phyllis Schlafly, Arthur Waldron, Robert Hill, Alex Acosta, Sen. Jon Kyl, Don Minter, Ovide Lamontagne, Matt Salmon, Tevi Troy, George Fondren, Roger Clegg, Thomas Fisher, Brendan Shields, John Nalbandian, Jeffrey Kemp, Alex Beehler, David Wurmser, Bill

Acknowledgments

Kristol, Chip Kahn, Ted Forstmann, Fred Smith, Tom Patterson, Jim Schlesinger, Reggie White, Angela Logomasini, Marlo Lewis, Doug Badger, Leonard Rabinowitz, Lisa Graham Keegan, R. J. Smith, Jesse Hernandez, Rick Richmond, Jim Gash, James Gattuso, Diana Furchtgott-Roth, Matthew Cunningham, Matthew Scully, Brian Hook, Kellyanne Fitzpatrick, Nancy Northcott, and Fred Davis.

Thanks to the people in my office who helped in many ways: Craig Whitney, Laura Minter, Angela Pritzl, Jennifer Hodges, Alex Vogel, Cameron Carter, Jared Belsher, Steve Thomlison, Julian Flannery, Lea Anne McBride, Lorie Nall, Ashley McGee, Wes Foster, Tracey Meyer, Wendi Rocci, Melissa Pezzetti, Phillip Stutts, Brian Nick, Andrew Kaplan, Carol Collett, Peggy Doven, Michael Turk, Jonathan Felts, Courtney Rang, Kevin Wright, Bill Wykpisz, Lisa Keller, Heather Conrad, and Connie Norsworthy.

Thanks also to Peter Robinson of the Hoover Institution, who helped with the early conception of the book and suggested its title.

My book agent, Sealy Yates, his colleague Tom Thompson, and the good folks at Word Publishing—Lee Gessner, Joey Paul, Laura Kendall, Jana Ford Muntsinger, Lanie Rockafellow, Pamela McClure, Allen Arnold, Sue Ann Jones, and Debbie Wickwire—saw the need for this book and made it happen in record time. I very much appreciate their professional competence and their enthusiastic encouragement.

Finally, the presence of Tucker, Ben, and Corinne in my life is a daily reminder of the need to keep fighting for their future. I am truly blessed.